Stress Management: 35 Transformative Techniques to Prevent and Reduce Everyday Stress in Your Life

Rami Georgiev

Published by Rami Georgiev, 2023.

STRESS MANAGEMENT: 35 TRANSFORMATIVE TECHNIQUES TO PREVENT AND REDUCE EVERYDAY STRESS IN YOUR LIFE

First edition. July 3, 2023.

ISBN: 979-8223725060

Written by Rami Georgiev.

In the midst of chaos, there is always a pathway to peace. Embrace the power within you to manage stress, cultivate calmness, and reclaim your inner balance. Rami Georgiev

Dedication:
For all the stressed souls,
whose days are filled with overwhelming demands,
whose minds are burdened with worry and anxiety,
whose hearts long for a moment of respite,
This book is dedicated to you.
May it be a guiding light, offering transformative techniques,
to prevent and reduce the everyday stress that weighs you down.
May you find solace, strength, and renewed hope,
as you embark on a journey of self-care and inner peace.
Remember, you have the power to reclaim your well-being,
and I stand with you in support and understanding.
You are deserving of a life filled with serenity and joy.
This book is for you.

Introduction: Understanding Stress: Causes, Effects, and Importance of Stress Management

In today's fast-paced world, stress has become a common companion in our lives. Understanding the nature of stress, its causes, effects, and the importance of stress management is crucial for leading a healthy and balanced life. In this chapter, we will explore the various aspects of stress and lay the foundation for effective stress management.

Causes of Stress

1. External Factors: Stress can arise from external sources such as work-related pressures, financial difficulties, relationship conflicts, major life changes, and environmental factors. These external stressors can trigger a response in our bodies and minds, leading to increased stress levels.

2. Internal Factors: Our own thoughts, perceptions, and beliefs can contribute to stress. Negative self-talk, perfectionism, unrealistic expectations, and excessive worry can create an internal environment that fosters stress and anxiety.

Effects of Stress

1. Physical Effects: Prolonged exposure to stress can have a significant impact on our physical health. It can lead to symptoms such as headaches, muscle tension, digestive problems, sleep disturbances, weakened immune system, and increased risk of chronic illnesses like heart disease and diabetes.

2. Emotional Effects: Stress can affect our emotional well-being, causing heightened levels of anxiety, irritability, mood swings, and feelings of being overwhelmed. It can also contribute to the

development or exacerbation of mental health conditions such as depression and anxiety disorders.

3. Cognitive Effects: Chronic stress can impair our cognitive functioning, affecting memory, concentration, and decision-making abilities. It may lead to mental fatigue, difficulty focusing, and decreased productivity. Additionally, stress can make it challenging to think clearly and problem-solve effectively.

Importance of Stress Management

1. Enhancing Overall Well-being: Stress management is vital for maintaining our overall well-being. By effectively managing stress, we can improve our physical health, emotional stability, and mental clarity. It allows us to lead a more balanced and fulfilling life.

2. Improving Relationships: Unmanaged stress can strain relationships, leading to conflicts and misunderstandings. By learning to manage stress, we can enhance our communication skills, reduce emotional reactivity, and cultivate healthier relationships with our loved ones.

3. Boosting Resilience: Stress management techniques help us build resilience and develop coping mechanisms to navigate challenges effectively. It equips us with the tools to handle stressors in a healthy and adaptive manner, reducing the negative impact on our lives.

4. Increasing Productivity and Performance: Chronic stress can hinder our productivity and performance in various areas of life, including work, education, and personal goals. Effective stress management techniques enable us to maintain focus, increase motivation, and perform at our best.

Conclusion

Understanding stress, its causes, effects, and the importance of stress management is the first step towards leading a healthier and more balanced life. By recognizing the factors that contribute to stress, acknowledging its impact on our physical and mental well-being, and embracing the significance of stress management, we can take proactive steps to reduce stress levels, improve our overall quality of life, and cultivate a sense of inner peace. In the following chapters, we will explore transformative techniques and strategies to effectively manage and reduce stress in our everyday lives.

Chapter 1: Mindfulness and Meditation Techniques

In our fast-paced and hectic world, practicing mindfulness and meditation can provide a much-needed sanctuary for the mind and soul. This chapter explores the transformative power of mindfulness and meditation techniques in managing stress, cultivating inner peace, and fostering overall well-being. By immersing ourselves in the present moment and embracing a state of calm awareness, we can navigate life's challenges with greater resilience and clarity.

Technique 1: Mindful Breathing

IN OUR FAST-PACED AND busy lives, finding moments of peace and tranquility can feel like a luxury. Mindful breathing offers a simple yet powerful practice that allows us to tap into a state of calm and centeredness, even amidst the chaos. This chapter explores the transformative practice of mindful breathing, its benefits, and how to incorporate it into our daily lives for stress reduction and enhanced well-being.

Understanding Mindful Breathing

Mindful breathing involves bringing our full attention to the act of breathing, observing each breath with curiosity and non-judgmental awareness. It is an ancient practice rooted in various mindfulness traditions, such as Buddhism and yoga, and has gained recognition for its effectiveness in reducing stress and promoting overall well-being.

The Practice of Mindful Breathing

1. Find a comfortable space: Choose a quiet and peaceful space where you can sit comfortably without distractions. You may choose to sit on a cushion, chair, or even on the floor with a meditation mat.

2. Get into a comfortable posture: Find a posture that allows you to be alert and relaxed. You can sit with your legs crossed, or if that's not comfortable, sit on a chair with your feet flat on the ground. Keep your back straight, but not rigid, and rest your hands comfortably on your lap.

3. Bring attention to your breath: Gently close your eyes or maintain a soft gaze, and shift your attention to your breath. Notice the sensation of the breath entering and leaving your body. You can focus on the rise and fall of your abdomen or the sensation of air passing through your nostrils.

4. Observe without judgment: As you continue to breathe, observe each breath without trying to change it. Notice the rhythm, depth, and quality of your breath. If your mind wanders, gently bring your attention back to the breath, without judgment or self-criticism.

5. Cultivate present moment awareness: Allow yourself to fully immerse in the present moment, anchored by the sensations of your breath. As thoughts, emotions, or sensations arise, acknowledge them without getting caught up in them. Simply return your focus to the breath, using it as an anchor to keep you grounded in the present.

Benefits of Mindful Breathing

1. Stress reduction: Mindful breathing activates the relaxation response in our bodies, calming the nervous system and reducing the physiological signs of stress. It helps to lower cortisol levels, reduce heart rate, and promote a sense of calmness and relaxation.

2. Increased self-awareness: By bringing attention to the breath, we develop a heightened sense of self-awareness. We become more attuned to our thoughts, emotions, and bodily sensations, allowing us to respond to stressors with greater clarity and self-compassion.

3. Improved focus and concentration: Mindful breathing enhances our ability to sustain focus and concentration. By training our attention to stay present with the breath, we cultivate the skill of concentration that can be applied to other areas of our lives, such as work, studies, or creative endeavors.

4. Emotional regulation: The practice of mindful breathing helps us develop emotional resilience. By observing our breath and staying present with our experiences, we learn to respond to emotions with greater awareness and compassion, rather than reacting impulsively or becoming overwhelmed by them.

Incorporating Mindful Breathing into Daily Life

Mindful breathing can be practiced anytime, anywhere, making it accessible for integration into our daily lives. Here are a few suggestions for incorporating mindful breathing into your routine:

- Morning practice: Start your day with a few minutes of mindful breathing to set a positive and centered tone for the day ahead.
- Mindful breaks: Take short breaks throughout the day to pause, close your eyes, and focus on a few mindful breaths. This can help you reset, regain focus, and reduce stress.
- Stressful situations: When faced with a challenging or stressful situation, take a moment to engage in mindful breathing before responding. This can help you approach the situation with greater clarity and calmness.
- Bedtime routine: Practice mindful breathing before going to bed to relax your body and quiet your mind, promoting better sleep and relaxation.

Conclusion

Mindful breathing is a powerful practice that brings us back to the present moment and supports our overall well-being. By incorporating mindful breathing into our daily lives, we can reduce stress, enhance self-awareness, improve focus, and cultivate emotional resilience. The simplicity and accessibility of mindful breathing make it a valuable tool for finding moments of peace and calm amidst the busyness of life.

Technique 2: Body Scan Meditation

IN OUR FAST-PACED AND often demanding lives, it's essential to carve out moments for relaxation and self-care. Body scan meditation offers a powerful practice that allows us to cultivate deep relaxation, body awareness, and a sense of inner peace. In this chapter, we will explore the transformative practice of body scan meditation, its benefits, and how to incorporate it into your daily routine for stress reduction and improved well-being.

Understanding Body Scan Meditation

Body scan meditation is a mindfulness practice that involves systematically directing our attention to different parts of the body, cultivating a deep sense of relaxation and awareness. It is a practice rooted in mindfulness-based stress reduction (MBSR) and has been widely recognized for its ability to reduce stress, release tension, and promote a greater connection between the mind and body.

The Practice of Body Scan Meditation

1. Find a comfortable position: Begin by finding a quiet and comfortable space where you can lie down or sit in a supported position. Make sure you can fully relax your body without any discomfort or strain.

2. Bring your attention to the body: Close your eyes or maintain a soft gaze. Start by bringing your awareness to your breath, allowing yourself to settle into the present moment.

3. Begin the scan: Slowly direct your attention to different parts of your body, starting from the top of your head and moving down to your toes. Notice any sensations, tension, or areas of tightness as you focus on each body part.

4. Cultivate awareness and relaxation: As you scan each body part, bring a gentle and non-judgmental awareness to any sensations you

encounter. If you notice tension or discomfort, bring your breath to that area, imagining it flowing through and releasing the tension. Allow the body to relax and soften with each breath.

5. Stay present with each body part: Take your time with each body part, spending a few moments observing and releasing any tension. If your mind wanders, gently guide your attention back to the body part you are focusing on, without judgment.

6. Complete the scan: Continue the body scan, moving through each part of your body until you reach your toes. Take a moment to embrace the overall sense of relaxation and connection with your body.

Benefits of Body Scan Meditation

1. Stress reduction: Body scan meditation promotes deep relaxation, allowing the body and mind to release accumulated stress and tension. It activates the body's relaxation response, helping to lower cortisol levels and promote a sense of calmness.

2. Body awareness: Through the practice of body scan meditation, we develop a heightened sense of body awareness. This increased awareness allows us to notice areas of tension or discomfort in our body, enabling us to address and release them.

3. Enhanced mind-body connection: Body scan meditation helps cultivate a deeper connection between the mind and body. By focusing our attention on each body part, we become more attuned to the sensations and messages our body is sending us, fostering a greater sense of self-care and self-compassion.

4. Improved relaxation and sleep: Regular practice of body scan meditation can contribute to better relaxation and improved sleep quality. By releasing tension and calming the mind, it creates a conducive environment for restful sleep and rejuvenation.

Incorporating Body Scan Meditation into Daily Life

Body scan meditation can be practiced at any time, but it is particularly beneficial during moments of stress or when you need to reconnect with your body and find inner calm. Here are some suggestions for incorporating body scan meditation into your daily routine:

- Morning or evening practice: Begin or end your day with a body scan meditation session to set a positive tone or unwind from the day's activities.

- Breaks throughout the day: Take short breaks during the day to engage in a brief body scan meditation. This can help you release tension, recenter yourself, and regain focus.

- Preparing for sleep: Practice a body scan meditation before bed to relax your body, calm your mind, and prepare yourself for a restful night's sleep.

Conclusion

Body scan meditation offers a pathway to deep relaxation, heightened body awareness, and a stronger mind-body connection. By incorporating this practice into your daily routine, you can reduce stress, release tension, and cultivate a greater sense of well-being. Embrace the opportunity to reconnect with your body, listen to its messages, and nourish yourself with the practice of body scan meditation.

Technique 3: Loving-Kindness Meditation

IN A WORLD THAT CAN sometimes feel disconnected and overwhelming, loving-kindness meditation offers a transformative practice that cultivates feelings of compassion, love, and kindness towards ourselves and others. This chapter explores the practice of loving-kindness meditation, its benefits, and how it can enrich our lives by fostering a deeper sense of connection, empathy, and well-being.

Understanding Loving-Kindness Meditation

Loving-kindness meditation, also known as metta meditation, is a contemplative practice rooted in ancient Buddhist traditions. It involves directing well-wishes and positive intentions towards ourselves, loved ones, acquaintances, and even those with whom we may have difficulties or conflicts. Through the repetition of affirmations and visualization, loving-kindness meditation helps expand our capacity for compassion and fosters a mindset of acceptance and understanding.

The Practice of Loving-Kindness Meditation

1. Find a comfortable position: Begin by finding a quiet and comfortable space where you can sit in a relaxed position. You can choose to sit on a cushion, chair, or even on the floor with a meditation mat. Allow your body to settle into a posture that is both alert and at ease.

2. Cultivate a loving and compassionate mindset: Close your eyes or maintain a soft gaze. Take a few moments to bring your attention to your heart center and cultivate a sense of warmth and loving-kindness within yourself. Take a few deep breaths, allowing yourself to relax and be present in the moment.

3. Set your intentions: Begin by directing loving-kindness towards yourself. Repeat affirmations or phrases that resonate with you, such as "May I be happy, may I be healthy, may I live with ease." Allow these intentions to resonate deeply within you, truly wishing yourself well-being and happiness.

4. Extend loving-kindness to others: Gradually expand your focus beyond yourself to loved ones, friends, acquaintances, and eventually all beings. Repeat the same affirmations or phrases for each group, visualizing them and sending them loving-kindness. For example, "May my loved ones be happy, may they be healthy, may they live with ease."

5. Embrace difficult relationships: As you become more comfortable with the practice, challenge yourself to extend loving-kindness towards those with whom you may have difficulties or conflicts. Recognize their humanity, their struggles, and offer them well-wishes with phrases like, "May [name of the person] be happy, may they be healthy, may they live with ease."

6. Expand your circle of compassion: In the final stage of the meditation, extend loving-kindness to all beings, near and far, known and unknown. Imagine your intentions spreading out like ripples in a pond, encompassing the entire world with love and compassion.

Benefits of Loving-Kindness Meditation

1. Cultivating compassion: Loving-kindness meditation cultivates a deep sense of compassion within ourselves. By directing positive intentions towards others, we develop a greater capacity for empathy, understanding, and connection.

2. Emotional well-being: The practice of loving-kindness meditation has been shown to reduce symptoms of depression, anxiety, and stress. It promotes positive emotions, such as happiness, gratitude, and love, which contribute to overall emotional well-being.

3. Improved relationships: Engaging in loving-kindness meditation enhances our ability to relate to others with kindness and empathy. It

strengthens relationships, fosters forgiveness, and encourages a more positive and harmonious social environment.

4. Self-compassion and self-acceptance: Loving-kindness meditation nurtures self-compassion and self-acceptance. By offering ourselves loving-kindness, we cultivate a deep sense of self-worth and develop a more compassionate relationship with ourselves.

Incorporating Loving-Kindness Meditation into Daily Life

Loving-kindness meditation can be practiced formally during dedicated meditation sessions, but its essence can also be integrated into daily life. Here are some suggestions for incorporating loving-kindness meditation into your routine:

- Morning intentions: Start your day by setting loving intentions for yourself and all beings you will encounter throughout the day.
- Daily reminders: Place notes or reminders in visible places to prompt acts of loving-kindness and compassion towards yourself and others.
- Challenging moments: When faced with difficulties or conflicts, pause and recite loving-kindness phrases to shift your mindset and approach the situation with compassion.
- Bedtime reflection: Reflect on the day before sleep, acknowledging moments of loving-kindness you shared with others and yourself.

Conclusion

Loving-kindness meditation is a profound practice that allows us to nurture compassion, empathy, and connection. By incorporating this practice into our lives, we can experience increased emotional well-being, improved relationships, and a greater sense of self-compassion. Embrace the power of loving-kindness meditation to cultivate love and kindness within yourself and share it with the world, fostering a more compassionate and harmonious existence.

Technique 4: Mindful Eating

IN OUR FAST-PACED MODERN society, we often find ourselves rushing through meals or mindlessly consuming food without fully savoring the experience. Mindful eating offers a powerful practice that invites us to slow down, reconnect with our bodies, and develop a healthier relationship with food. In this chapter, we explore the practice of mindful eating, its benefits, and how it can transform our eating habits for improved well-being.

Understanding Mindful Eating

Mindful eating is an approach that involves paying deliberate attention to the present moment and engaging all our senses while eating. It encourages us to observe the colors, textures, flavors, and aromas of our food, as well as the physical sensations and emotions that arise during the eating process. By bringing awareness to our eating habits, we can make conscious choices and develop a deeper appreciation for nourishing our bodies.

The Practice of Mindful Eating

1. Create a calm eating environment: Find a quiet and pleasant space to enjoy your meal. Remove distractions like electronic devices, TV, or work-related materials. Set the table mindfully, creating an inviting and peaceful atmosphere.

2. Engage your senses: Before taking your first bite, take a moment to observe the appearance, colors, and arrangement of the food on your plate. Take a deep breath and notice the aromas that emanate from the meal. Pay attention to the textures and shapes of the food as you take each bite.

3. Eat slowly and savor each bite: Take small bites and chew slowly, allowing yourself to fully experience the taste and texture of the food. Notice the flavors, the way the food changes as you chew, and the sensations it creates in your mouth.

4. Tune in to your body's signals: Throughout the meal, periodically check in with your body's hunger and fullness cues. Notice

the physical sensations of hunger and satiety, and eat until you feel comfortably satisfied, rather than overly full.

5. Cultivate gratitude: Take a moment to express gratitude for the food you are about to eat. Reflect on the effort and care that went into its preparation, as well as the nourishment it provides for your body.

6. Non-judgmental awareness: Approach your eating experience with curiosity and non-judgmental awareness. Notice any thoughts or emotions that arise during the meal without attaching labels of "good" or "bad." Accept and acknowledge them, allowing them to pass without judgment.

Benefits of Mindful Eating

1. Enhanced enjoyment and satisfaction: By slowing down and savoring each bite, we can fully appreciate the flavors and textures of our food, leading to a heightened sense of enjoyment and satisfaction.

2. Improved digestion and nutrient absorption: Eating mindfully allows our bodies to fully engage in the digestive process. By chewing food thoroughly and being present while eating, we promote optimal digestion and nutrient absorption.

3. Better portion control and weight management: Mindful eating promotes a greater awareness of portion sizes and helps us distinguish between physical hunger and emotional or mindless eating. This awareness can support healthy weight management and prevent overeating.

4. Reduced emotional eating: By bringing awareness to our emotions and the triggers that lead to emotional eating, we can develop a healthier relationship with food and find alternative ways to cope with emotions.

Incorporating Mindful Eating into Daily Life

Mindful eating can be practiced in various ways throughout the day. Here are some suggestions for incorporating it into your daily routine:

- Choose one meal or snack per day to eat mindfully, dedicating your full attention to the experience.

- Take a moment to pause and breathe before eating, bringing yourself into the present moment and setting an intention for mindful eating.

- Practice gratitude before and after each meal, expressing appreciation for the nourishment you receive.

Conclusion

Mindful eating offers us an opportunity to reconnect with the present moment, cultivate a deeper appreciation for food, and develop a healthier relationship with eating. By engaging our senses, slowing down, and listening to our bodies, we can transform our eating habits and promote overall well-being. Embrace the practice of mindful eating as a pathway to nourishing not just your body, but also your mind and spirit.

Technique 5: Mindful Walking

IN OUR FAST-PACED LIVES, we often rush from one place to another without fully experiencing the simple act of walking. Mindful walking invites us to slow down, reconnect with our bodies, and find moments of peace and presence in our daily movements. This chapter explores the practice of mindful walking, its benefits, and how it can bring greater awareness and serenity to our lives.

Understanding Mindful Walking

Mindful walking is a practice that involves bringing full attention to the act of walking, engaging our senses, and connecting with our surroundings. It is an opportunity to shift from autopilot mode to a state of mindful awareness, where each step becomes a conscious act of presence. Mindful walking can be practiced both indoors and outdoors, offering a chance to experience the present moment in motion.

The Practice of Mindful Walking

1. Choose your walking environment: Find a quiet and peaceful place where you can walk without distractions. It can be a park, a garden, a beach, or any location that allows you to connect with nature or find tranquility.

2. Begin with intention: Before you start walking, take a moment to set your intention for the practice. It can be as simple as wanting to be fully present or cultivating a sense of gratitude for the opportunity to walk.

3. Tune into your body: As you start walking, bring your attention to the sensations in your body. Notice the contact of your feet with the ground, the movement of your legs, and the rhythm of your breath. Be

aware of the muscles involved in each step and the sensations of balance and coordination.

4. Engage your senses: Allow your senses to come alive as you walk. Notice the sights around you, the colors, shapes, and textures of the environment. Listen to the sounds of nature or the cityscape, whether it's the rustling of leaves, the chirping of birds, or the bustling of people. Feel the air on your skin, the temperature, and any subtle sensations that arise.

5. Stay present with each step: Focus your attention on the act of walking itself. Feel the weight shifting from one foot to the other, the sensations in your feet and legs, and the gentle movement of your body. Be fully present with each step, allowing the natural rhythm of your walking to guide you.

6. Cultivate gratitude and awareness: As you walk, practice gratitude for your body's ability to move and for the world around you. Notice the beauty in the simplest things, such as the patterns on tree bark or the gentle breeze against your face. Be open to the present moment and allow it to unfold with curiosity and wonder.

Benefits of Mindful Walking

1. Stress reduction and relaxation: Mindful walking provides a break from the constant mental chatter and can help reduce stress levels. It offers an opportunity to relax, rejuvenate, and find moments of calm in the midst of a busy day.

2. Improved focus and concentration: By focusing on the sensations of walking, mindful walking enhances your ability to stay present and cultivate concentration. It can be a valuable practice for training the mind to be more focused and attentive.

3. Connection with nature: Walking mindfully in nature allows you to connect with the natural world around you. It fosters a sense of interconnectedness and appreciation for the beauty and serenity of the environment.

4. Enhanced body awareness: Mindful walking brings awareness to the physical sensations of walking, promoting a deeper connection with your body. It can improve balance, posture, and overall body awareness.

Incorporating Mindful Walking into Daily Life

Mindful walking can be integrated into your daily life, whether you have a dedicated walking practice or simply incorporate moments of mindfulness during your usual walks. Here are some suggestions for incorporating mindful walking into your routine

- START YOUR DAY WITH a mindful walk: Begin your morning with a short mindful walk to set a positive tone for the day. Focus on the sensations of each step and the beauty of your surroundings.
- Walking meditation: Instead of sitting for meditation, take your practice outdoors and engage in a walking meditation. Walk slowly, intentionally, and bring your attention to the present moment.
- Walking breaks: During your workday or when you need a break from a sedentary routine, take short mindful walking breaks. Step outside, breathe in fresh air, and walk mindfully for a few minutes to recharge and reset.

Conclusion

Mindful walking is a gentle yet profound practice that allows us to bring mindfulness into our movements and discover moments of peace and presence in our daily lives. By walking with intention, engaging our senses, and staying fully present, we can cultivate a deeper connection with ourselves, our bodies, and the world around us. Embrace the practice of mindful walking as a powerful way to integrate mindfulness into your daily routine and experience the transformative benefits it offers.

Chapter 2: Physical Exercise for Stress Relief

Physical exercise is a powerful tool for managing and reducing stress. Engaging in regular exercise not only benefits our physical health but also has a profound impact on our mental and emotional well-being. In this chapter, we explore the connection between physical exercise and stress relief, along with various exercise techniques that can help you prevent and reduce stress in your life.

PHYSICAL EXERCISE TRIGGERS the release of endorphins, which are natural chemicals in the brain that promote feelings of well-being and happiness. Exercise also increases the production of neurotransmitters like serotonin and norepinephrine, which play a crucial role in regulating mood and reducing stress. Additionally, engaging in exercise provides an outlet for releasing pent-up energy and tension, promoting relaxation and a sense of accomplishment.

Technique 6: Cardiovascular Exercises for Stress Relief

CARDIOVASCULAR EXERCISES, also known as aerobic exercises, are activities that elevate your heart rate and get your blood pumping. These exercises have numerous benefits for both physical and mental well-being, including their ability to reduce stress. In this section, we explore various cardiovascular exercises that can help you manage and alleviate stress in your life.

Understanding Cardiovascular Exercises

Cardiovascular exercises involve repetitive movements that engage large muscle groups and increase your heart rate. These exercises improve cardiovascular fitness, boost mood, and release endorphins, which are natural stress-fighting chemicals in the brain. By incorporating cardiovascular exercises into your routine, you can experience the stress-relieving benefits and promote overall health.

Different Types of Cardiovascular Exercises

1. Jogging/Running: Jogging or running is a popular cardiovascular exercise that can be done outdoors or on a treadmill. It increases your heart rate, improves cardiovascular endurance, and releases endorphins, promoting a sense of well-being and stress relief.

2. Brisk Walking: Brisk walking is a low-impact cardiovascular exercise that is accessible to people of all fitness levels. It involves walking at a faster pace than usual, raising your heart rate and improving blood circulation. Take a brisk walk in nature or around your neighborhood to enjoy the added benefits of fresh air and scenery.

3. Cycling: Whether you prefer outdoor cycling or stationary biking, cycling is an excellent cardiovascular exercise that strengthens your legs, improves cardiovascular fitness, and reduces stress. Enjoy the freedom of exploring new routes outdoors or join a spin class for a group exercise experience.

4. Swimming: Swimming is a low-impact, full-body workout that is gentle on the joints. It provides resistance to your muscles while keeping you cool and refreshed. The rhythmic movements and focus on breathing in the water create a calming and meditative experience, making swimming an ideal stress-relieving exercise.

5. Dance Aerobics: Dance aerobics combines cardiovascular exercise with rhythmic movements and music, making it a fun and

enjoyable way to relieve stress. Join a dance fitness class or follow online dance workouts to get your heart rate up and let loose.

6. High-Intensity Interval Training (HIIT): HIIT workouts involve short bursts of intense exercise followed by periods of rest or lower-intensity activity. These workouts can be done with bodyweight exercises, equipment, or cardio exercises like burpees, jumping jacks, or mountain climbers. HIIT training not only improves cardiovascular fitness but also releases endorphins, helping you combat stress.

7. Group Fitness Classes: Joining group fitness classes like Zumba, kickboxing, or step aerobics can be a fantastic way to engage in cardiovascular exercise while enjoying the energy and motivation of a group setting. The social aspect of group classes adds an extra dimension of stress relief and enjoyment.

Incorporating Cardiovascular Exercises into Your Routine

To make cardiovascular exercises a regular part of your stress management routine, consider the following tips:

- Start slowly and gradually increase the intensity and duration of your workouts to avoid overexertion.
- Find activities that you enjoy and that fit your preferences and lifestyle. Experiment with different exercises to keep things interesting.
- Schedule your workouts at times when you are most likely to stick to them consistently.
- Mix up your exercises to challenge different muscle groups and prevent boredom.
- Listen to your body and take rest days when needed to avoid burnout or injury.
- Consider incorporating cardiovascular exercises into your daily routine, such as walking or biking to work or taking the stairs instead of the elevator.

Conclusion

Cardiovascular exercises provide an effective and enjoyable way to manage and reduce stress in your life. By engaging in activities that elevate your heart rate, release endorphins, and improve overall fitness, you can experience the physical, mental, and emotional benefits of stress relief. Find the cardiovascular exercises that resonate with you and incorporate them into your routine to promote a healthier, more balanced lifestyle.

Technique 7: Strength Training and Yoga for Stress Relief

STRENGTH TRAINING AND yoga are two powerful forms of exercise that offer unique benefits for stress relief. While strength training helps build physical strength and resilience, yoga combines physical movement, breath control, and mindfulness to promote relaxation and inner peace. In this chapter, we explore the role of strength training and yoga in managing stress and enhancing overall well-being.

Strength Training for Stress Relief

Strength training involves performing exercises that target specific muscle groups to build strength, endurance, and flexibility. While the primary focus of strength training is physical fitness, it also offers significant benefits for stress relief. Here's how strength training can help reduce stress:

1. Release of Endorphins: Like cardiovascular exercises, strength training stimulates the release of endorphins in the brain. These natural chemicals promote feelings of happiness, reduce pain, and enhance overall well-being, providing a natural and effective stress relief.

2. Sense of Accomplishment: Setting goals, tracking progress, and achieving strength milestones can boost self-confidence and provide a sense of accomplishment. The process of challenging oneself physically and achieving desired results can have a positive impact on mental and emotional well-being, counteracting the effects of stress.

3. Channeling Energy: Strength training provides an outlet for releasing pent-up energy and tension. By engaging in intense physical activity, you can channel your energy in a productive and healthy way, helping to alleviate stress and promote a sense of calm.

4. Improved Sleep Quality: Regular strength training has been shown to improve sleep quality, which is essential for stress management. Better sleep allows the body to recover and rejuvenate, reducing the impact of stress on physical and mental health.

Yoga for Stress Relief

Yoga is a mind-body practice that combines physical postures (asanas), breath control (pranayama), and meditation to promote overall well-being. Its holistic approach makes it an effective tool for stress relief. Here are the ways yoga can help reduce stress:

1. Relaxation Response: Practicing yoga activates the parasympathetic nervous system, triggering the body's relaxation response. Through deep breathing, gentle movements, and mindful awareness, yoga promotes a state of calm and relaxation, counteracting the stress response.

2. Mindfulness and Stress Reduction: Yoga encourages the cultivation of mindfulness, which involves bringing full attention to the present moment without judgment. By focusing on the sensations of the body, the breath, and the present experience, yoga helps to quiet the mind, reduce stress, and promote a sense of inner peace.

3. Stress Hormone Regulation: Research has shown that regular yoga practice can regulate stress hormones such as cortisol, reducing their levels in the body. By bringing balance to the endocrine system, yoga helps to counteract the harmful effects of chronic stress on physical and mental health.

4. Body Awareness and Self-Care: Yoga cultivates a deep connection between the body, mind, and breath. Through practicing yoga, you develop a heightened sense of body awareness, allowing you

to recognize and address areas of tension or stress in your body. This awareness promotes self-care and supports overall well-being.

Incorporating Strength Training and Yoga into Your Routine

To make strength training and yoga a regular part of your stress management routine, consider the following tips:

- Set specific goals: Whether it's increasing the amount of weight you lift in strength training or mastering a challenging yoga pose, set specific goals to keep yourself motivated and track your progress.
- Find a balance: Alternate between strength training and yoga sessions to benefit from the unique advantages each offers. This balance allows you to build physical strength while promoting relaxation and mindfulness.
- Seek guidance: If you're new to strength training or yoga, consider working with a qualified instructor who can guide you through proper techniques and help you design a safe and effective program.
- Practice mindfulness: Approach your strength training and yoga sessions with a mindful attitude. Focus on your breath, stay present in the moment, and listen to your body's signals. This mindful approach enhances the stress-relieving benefits of these practices.

Conclusion

Strength training and yoga offer valuable tools for managing and reducing stress in your life. By incorporating these practices into your routine, you can build physical strength, improve flexibility, cultivate mindfulness, and promote a sense of inner peace. Find a balance that works for you and reap the benefits of these transformative exercises in your journey towards stress-free living.

Technique 8: Outdoor Activities and Nature Connection for Stress Relief

ENGAGING IN OUTDOOR activities and connecting with nature is a powerful way to reduce stress and enhance overall well-being. The healing qualities of nature, combined with physical movement and fresh air, provide a unique opportunity to rejuvenate the mind, body, and spirit. In this chapter, we explore the benefits of outdoor activities and how connecting with nature can help alleviate stress.

The Healing Power of Nature

Nature has a profound impact on our well-being. Spending time outdoors and immersing ourselves in natural environments can:

1. Reduce Stress: Nature has a calming effect on the mind and body. Being surrounded by natural elements such as trees, water, and open spaces can help reduce cortisol levels (the stress hormone) and promote a sense of tranquility.

2. Enhance Mood: Nature exposure is associated with improved mood and increased feelings of happiness and relaxation. The beauty and serenity of natural settings can uplift our spirits and provide a refreshing break from the demands of daily life.

3. Restore Attention and Mental Fatigue: Spending time in nature can help restore our attention and mental energy. The soothing qualities of natural environments allow our minds to relax and recharge, reducing mental fatigue and improving focus.

Outdoor Activities for Stress Relief

1. Hiking and Trail Walking: Explore hiking trails and immerse yourself in the beauty of nature. Hiking allows you to engage in physical activity while enjoying the serenity of natural surroundings. It promotes cardiovascular health, releases endorphins, and provides a sense of accomplishment.

2. Gardening: Connect with nature by tending to a garden. Gardening offers a peaceful and therapeutic experience, allowing you to reconnect with the earth and nurture living plants. It provides an opportunity to engage in physical activity, cultivate mindfulness, and witness the beauty of growth and renewal.

3. Forest Bathing: Forest bathing, or Shinrin-yoku, is a Japanese practice of immersing oneself in a forest environment. It involves

mindfully observing nature, breathing in the forest air, and allowing the senses to be fully present. Forest bathing has been shown to reduce stress, lower blood pressure, and boost immune function.

4. Water Activities: Engage in water-based activities such as swimming, kayaking, paddleboarding, or simply relaxing by the beach. The calming effect of water, combined with the physical movement and exposure to natural elements, can promote relaxation and stress relief.

5. Cycling and Biking: Explore scenic routes and enjoy the benefits of outdoor cycling. Biking allows you to cover more ground, experience the beauty of nature, and engage in a cardiovascular workout. It can be an invigorating and enjoyable way to reduce stress and improve overall fitness.

6. Nature Photography: Capture the beauty of nature through photography. Going on nature walks with the intention of photographing the surroundings encourages you to slow down, observe the details, and appreciate the natural world. Nature photography combines creativity, mindfulness, and the therapeutic effects of being in nature.

Connecting with Nature for Stress Relief

1. Mindful Observation: Practice mindful observation by immersing yourself in nature and paying attention to the sights, sounds, and sensations around you. Take the time to notice the colors, textures, and movements of the natural world. Engaging your senses in this way promotes presence and mindfulness.

2. Nature Meditation: Find a quiet spot in nature where you can sit or lie down comfortably. Close your eyes or soften your gaze and focus on your breath. Allow the sounds, smells, and sensations of nature to guide your meditation practice, deepening your connection with the natural environment.

3. Nature Journaling: Keep a nature journal to record your experiences, observations, and reflections while spending time outdoors. Write about the sights, sounds, and feelings that nature

evokes in you. Nature journaling promotes self-expression, mindfulness, and a deeper appreciation for the natural world.

Incorporating Outdoor Activities and Nature Connection into Your Routine

To make outdoor activities and nature connection a regular part of your stress management routine, consider the following tips:

- Schedule outdoor time: Set aside dedicated time each week to engage in outdoor activities or simply spend time in nature. Treat it as a non-negotiable part of your self-care routine.

- Explore new environments: Venture beyond your usual surroundings and explore different natural environments. Visit parks, forests, beaches, or mountains in your area to experience the diversity and beauty of nature.

- Unplug and disconnect: When engaging in outdoor activities, disconnect from electronic devices and immerse yourself fully in the natural experience. Allow yourself to be present in the moment and fully engage with the surroundings.

- Practice gratitude: Cultivate a sense of gratitude for the natural world. Take time to appreciate the beauty and wonder of nature, expressing gratitude for its healing powers and the joy it brings to your life.

Conclusion

Outdoor activities and connecting with nature offer a powerful antidote to stress and promote overall well-being. By immersing yourself in natural environments, engaging in physical activity, and cultivating a deeper connection with the natural world, you can experience the rejuvenating effects of nature and find solace in its tranquility. Embrace the healing power of outdoor activities and let nature be your guide in your journey towards stress relief and inner peace.

Chapter 3: Effective Time Management and Prioritization

Time is a precious resource, and how we manage it has a significant impact on our stress levels and overall well-being. In this chapter, we delve into the importance of effective time management and prioritization as key strategies for reducing stress and increasing productivity. By understanding how to make the most of your time and aligning your priorities, you can create a sense of balance and control in your life. Time management is about making conscious choices regarding how we spend our time. It involves setting priorities, allocating time to different tasks, and finding strategies to optimize productivity.

Technique 9: Setting SMART Goals for Effective Time Management

SETTING GOALS IS A fundamental aspect of effective time management. When our actions align with clear and well-defined goals, we can prioritize our tasks, stay focused, and make efficient use of our time. In this section, we explore the concept of SMART goals and how they can contribute to effective time management and stress reduction.

Understanding SMART Goals

SMART is an acronym that stands for Specific, Measurable, Achievable, Relevant, and Time-bound. Setting SMART goals ensures that your goals are well-defined, attainable, and have a clear timeline. Here's a breakdown of each component:

1. Specific: Your goal should be clear and concise. Clearly define what you want to achieve and why it is important to you. The more specific your goal, the easier it is to plan and take action.

Example: Instead of setting a vague goal like "Improve my fitness," make it more specific by saying "Run a half marathon in six months."

2. Measurable: Establish criteria for measuring your progress and success. Having quantifiable measures helps you track your progress, stay motivated, and make adjustments as needed.

Example: Instead of saying "Get better at public speaking," make it measurable by saying "Deliver a presentation to a group of 50 people without any significant anxiety."

3. Achievable: Ensure that your goal is realistic and attainable within your capabilities. Consider your resources, skills, and time constraints. Setting achievable goals increases your confidence, motivation, and likelihood of success.

Example: Instead of setting an overwhelming goal like "Learn five new languages in a year," make it more achievable by saying "Learn the basics of one new language within six months."

4. Relevant: Your goal should align with your overall objectives and aspirations. Make sure it is meaningful and relevant to your personal or professional growth. A relevant goal will provide a sense of purpose and drive.

Example: Instead of setting a goal that doesn't align with your interests, such as "Learn to play the guitar," set a relevant goal like "Learn to play classical guitar pieces to enhance my musical skills."

5. Time-bound: Set a specific timeframe or deadline for achieving your goal. This creates a sense of urgency and helps you stay focused. A time-bound goal provides a clear target to work towards.

Example: Instead of setting an open-ended goal like "Write a book someday," make it time-bound by saying "Complete the first draft of my book within six months."

Benefits of Setting SMART Goals for Time Management

Setting SMART goals enhances time management in several ways:

1. Clarity and Focus: SMART goals provide clarity by defining exactly what you want to achieve. This clarity helps you prioritize your tasks and allocate time accordingly, ensuring that you stay focused on the most important activities.

2. Motivation and Accountability: SMART goals give you a clear target to strive for, keeping you motivated and accountable for your progress. When you can measure your achievements, you're more likely to stay committed and take consistent action.

3. Efficient Resource Allocation: By setting achievable and relevant goals, you can allocate your time and resources effectively. You avoid wasting time on tasks that don't align with your goals and can focus on activities that bring you closer to success.

4. Improved Planning and Time Estimation: SMART goals require you to consider the time needed to achieve them. This helps you plan your tasks more effectively, estimate how long each task will take, and create realistic schedules.

Conclusion

Setting SMART goals is a powerful strategy for effective time management. By making your goals Specific, Measurable, Achievable, Relevant, and Time-bound, you create a roadmap for success, enhance your focus, and maximize your productivity. Incorporate SMART goal-setting into your time management practices, and experience the benefits of increased clarity, motivation, and progress towards your desired outcomes.

Technique 10: Creating a Daily and Weekly Schedule for Effective Time Management

CREATING A WELL-STRUCTURED daily and weekly schedule is essential for effective time management. A carefully planned schedule helps you prioritize tasks, manage your time efficiently, and reduce stress by providing a sense of structure and control. In this section, we explore the importance of creating a schedule and provide practical tips for designing a daily and weekly routine that optimizes your productivity and well-being.

The Benefits of a Schedule

A well-designed schedule offers numerous benefits:

1. Organization: A schedule provides a clear overview of your tasks, commitments, and priorities. It helps you stay organized and ensures that you don't overlook important deadlines or responsibilities.

2. Time Allocation: By creating a schedule, you can allocate specific time slots for each task or activity. This ensures that you have dedicated time for essential tasks, as well as for self-care, relaxation, and pursuing your personal interests.

3. Productivity: A schedule helps you manage your time more effectively, minimizing distractions and procrastination. By having a plan in place, you can focus on the most important tasks and make efficient use of your available time.

4. Stress Reduction: Knowing what to expect and having a clear plan in place reduces uncertainty and stress. A well-structured schedule provides a sense of control, allowing you to approach your tasks with confidence and peace of mind.

Tips for Creating a Daily and Weekly Schedule

1. Identify Priorities: Start by identifying your most important tasks and obligations. These may include work-related responsibilities, personal goals, and self-care activities. Rank them in order of importance.

2. Allocate Time Blocks: Assign specific time blocks for each task or activity. Be realistic about how long each task will take and consider

your peak energy levels during the day. Leave some buffer time between tasks to account for unforeseen circumstances or breaks.

3. Create a Routine: Establish a consistent daily routine that incorporates regular activities such as waking up, meal times, exercise, and relaxation. Having a predictable routine helps you maintain a sense of structure and reduces decision-making fatigue.

4. Utilize Productivity Techniques: Incorporate productivity techniques such as time blocking, Pomodoro technique (working in focused bursts with breaks), or the 80/20 rule (focusing on tasks that yield the most significant results). Experiment with different techniques to find what works best for you.

5. Be Flexible: While a schedule provides structure, it's important to remain flexible. Unexpected events or changes in priorities may arise. Allow room for adjustments and be willing to adapt your schedule accordingly.

6. Prioritize Self-Care: Make self-care activities a non-negotiable part of your schedule. Allocate time for activities that nourish your physical, mental, and emotional well-being, such as exercise, meditation, hobbies, and spending time with loved ones.

7. Avoid Overloading: Be mindful not to over-schedule yourself. Leave some breathing room in your schedule to account for breaks, relaxation, and unplanned activities. Avoid the temptation to fill every minute of your day with tasks, as this can lead to burnout and decreased productivity.

8. Regularly Review and Adjust: Review your schedule regularly to assess its effectiveness and make necessary adjustments. Reflect on what worked well and what needs improvement. As your priorities and circumstances change, adapt your schedule accordingly.

Conclusion

Creating a daily and weekly schedule is a valuable tool for effective time management. It helps you prioritize tasks, allocate time wisely, and reduce stress by providing structure and organization. By implementing these tips and designing a schedule that aligns with your goals and values, you can optimize your productivity, balance your responsibilities, and enhance your overall well-being. Embrace the power of a well-planned schedule and experience the benefits of improved time management.

Technique 11: Prioritizing Tasks and Eliminating Time Wasters for Effective Time Management

EFFECTIVE TIME MANAGEMENT involves not only creating a schedule but also prioritizing tasks and eliminating time wasters. Prioritization allows you to focus on the most important and high-impact activities, while eliminating time wasters helps you reclaim valuable time and increase productivity. In this section, we explore techniques for prioritizing tasks and strategies for identifying and eliminating common time wasters.

Prioritizing Tasks

1. Identify Important Tasks: Start by identifying tasks that align with your goals and have the most significant impact on your desired outcomes. These tasks should contribute to your long-term success and bring you closer to your objectives.

2. Use Prioritization Methods: There are several prioritization methods you can employ, such as the Eisenhower Matrix, the ABC Method, or the MoSCoW Technique. Choose a method that resonates with you and helps you differentiate between urgent and important tasks.

3. Consider Deadlines and Time Sensitivity: Take into account the deadlines or time sensitivity of tasks. Focus on tasks with approaching deadlines or those that require immediate attention.

4. Evaluate Effort and Impact: Assess the effort required for each task and the potential impact it will have on your goals. Prioritize tasks that offer high impact while considering the effort involved.

5. Reassess and Adjust: Regularly reassess your priorities as circumstances change. Adjust your task list and schedule accordingly to ensure that you stay focused on the most relevant and time-sensitive activities.

Eliminating Time Wasters

1. Identify Common Time Wasters: Reflect on activities or habits that consume your time without contributing to your goals or well-being. These can include excessive social media use, excessive email checking, multitasking, or unnecessary meetings.

2. Set Boundaries: Establish boundaries to protect your time and minimize distractions. For example, limit social media usage to specific times of the day or set aside designated periods for email checking.

3. Delegate and Outsource: Delegate tasks that can be handled by others, freeing up your time for more important responsibilities. Consider outsourcing tasks that are outside your expertise or consume a significant amount of time.

4. Practice Time Blocking: Allocate specific time blocks for focused work on important tasks. During these blocks, eliminate distractions and fully commit to the task at hand.

5. Learn to Say No: Be selective about accepting additional commitments or tasks that do not align with your priorities. Learn to say no graciously to requests that would stretch your time and energy thin.

6. Streamline and Automate: Look for ways to streamline your workflows and automate repetitive tasks. Utilize technology tools and applications that can help automate processes and save you time.

7. Take Breaks: Paradoxically, taking regular breaks can improve productivity. Allow yourself short breaks between tasks to recharge and maintain focus.

Conclusion

Prioritizing tasks and eliminating time wasters are crucial steps in effective time management. By identifying and focusing on important tasks, you can allocate your time wisely and make progress towards your goals. Simultaneously, by eliminating time wasters and establishing boundaries, you can reclaim valuable time and increase productivity. Embrace these strategies, and experience the benefits of improved focus, efficiency, and a sense of accomplishment in your daily life.

Technique 12: Delegating and Seeking Support for Effective Time Management

ONE OF THE KEY PRINCIPLES of effective time management is recognizing that you don't have to do everything yourself. Delegating tasks and seeking support from others can help you optimize your time, reduce overwhelm, and focus on your core responsibilities. In this section, we explore the importance of delegation and strategies for effectively delegating tasks and seeking support when needed.

The Benefits of Delegation

1. Time Optimization: Delegating tasks allows you to leverage the skills and capabilities of others, freeing up your time to focus on high-value activities that require your expertise. It enables you to allocate your time more efficiently and effectively.

2. Enhanced Productivity: Delegating tasks to individuals who are better suited or more skilled in those areas can lead to increased productivity. It allows each team member to work on tasks that align with their strengths, resulting in higher-quality outcomes and faster completion.

3. Skill Development: Delegation provides an opportunity for others to develop new skills and grow professionally. By assigning tasks that challenge and stretch their abilities, you foster a culture of learning and development within your team or organization.

4. Collaboration and Teamwork: Delegation promotes collaboration and teamwork. It encourages individuals to work together, share knowledge, and support one another in achieving common goals. It fosters a sense of camaraderie and collective success.

Strategies for Effective Delegation

1. Assess Task Suitability: Evaluate the tasks on your plate and identify those that can be delegated without compromising quality or outcomes. Consider the skills, expertise, and availability of potential team members or colleagues who can take on those tasks.

2. Clearly Define Expectations: When delegating tasks, clearly communicate your expectations regarding outcomes, timelines, and quality standards. Provide all necessary information, resources, and context to ensure a smooth handover.

3. Match Skills and Abilities: Delegate tasks to individuals who have the skills, knowledge, and capacity to handle them effectively. Consider their strengths and interests to ensure a good match between the task and the person responsible.

4. Provide Support and Guidance: Offer support and guidance to the individuals you delegate tasks to. Be available to answer questions, provide clarification, and offer assistance when needed. This helps build confidence and ensures successful task completion.

5. Foster Accountability: Establish clear accountability measures to track progress and ensure timely completion of delegated tasks. Regular check-ins, progress updates, and feedback sessions can help maintain accountability and provide opportunities for course correction if necessary.

6. Recognize and Appreciate Efforts: Acknowledge the contributions of individuals who successfully complete delegated tasks. Express your gratitude and provide positive feedback to encourage continued engagement and motivation.

Seeking Support

1. Identify Areas of Support: Recognize areas where you can benefit from external support. This could be seeking assistance from colleagues, outsourcing specific tasks to experts, or partnering with individuals who complement your skill set.

2. Communicate Your Needs: Clearly communicate your needs to those you seek support from. Articulate the tasks or areas where you require assistance, along with any specific expectations or deadlines.

3. Build a Support Network: Cultivate relationships with individuals who can provide support and guidance in different aspects of your life. This network can include mentors, coaches, colleagues, or friends who can offer advice, expertise, or emotional support when needed.

4. Practice Effective Communication: When seeking support, be clear and concise in your communication. Provide context, be specific about your needs, and maintain open lines of communication to ensure a smooth collaboration.

Conclusion

Delegating tasks and seeking support are essential strategies for effective time management. By delegating tasks, you can optimize your time, enhance productivity, and foster a collaborative work environment. Similarly, by seeking support, you can tap into the expertise and resources of others, enabling you to accomplish more and achieve better outcomes. Embrace these strategies and enjoy the benefits of increased productivity, reduced stress, and a more balanced approach to managing your time.

Chapter 4: Journaling and Emotional Release Techniques for Stress Management

Journaling and emotional release techniques are powerful tools for managing stress and enhancing emotional well-being. They provide a safe and private space for self-reflection, self-expression, and processing emotions. In this section, we explore the benefits of journaling and various techniques that can help you release and manage your emotions effectively.

The Benefits of Journaling

Emotional Expression: Journaling offers a healthy outlet for expressing and processing emotions. It provides a space to unload and release pent-up feelings, reducing emotional stress and promoting emotional well-being.

Self-Reflection and Insight: Through journaling, you can gain valuable insights about yourself, your thoughts, and your emotions. It helps you develop self-awareness and a deeper understanding of your experiences, allowing you to make positive changes and grow personally.

Stress Reduction: Writing in a journal can help alleviate stress by allowing you to unload and make sense of overwhelming emotions. It provides a sense of release and relief, promoting relaxation and a greater sense of calm.

Problem Solving: Journaling can be a tool for problem-solving and decision-making. Writing about challenges or dilemmas can help you gain clarity, identify patterns, and explore possible solutions.

Tracking Progress: Keeping a journal enables you to track your progress over time. You can review past entries and observe patterns, setbacks, and growth, providing motivation and encouragement.

Technique 13: Gratitude Journaling for Cultivating Positivity and Well-being

GRATITUDE JOURNALING is a simple yet powerful practice that can significantly enhance your overall well-being and mindset. By regularly acknowledging and appreciating the things you are grateful for, you can shift your focus to the positive aspects of your life, increase happiness, and cultivate a sense of contentment. In this section, we delve into the benefits of gratitude journaling and provide guidance on how to incorporate this practice into your daily life.

The Benefits of Gratitude Journaling

1. Positive Mindset: Gratitude journaling helps reframe your mindset by shifting your focus from what is lacking to what you already have. It trains your mind to seek out and appreciate the positive aspects of your life, fostering a more optimistic and grateful outlook.

2. Increased Happiness: Cultivating gratitude has been linked to increased levels of happiness and life satisfaction. By consistently acknowledging and expressing gratitude, you can experience a greater sense of fulfillment and contentment.

3. Stress Reduction: Practicing gratitude can help reduce stress levels. When you focus on the things you are grateful for, it shifts your attention away from stressors and promotes relaxation. It can also provide a sense of perspective and resilience when faced with challenges.

4. Improved Relationships: Expressing gratitude towards others strengthens relationships and fosters a sense of connection. By acknowledging and appreciating the kindness and support you receive, you deepen your bonds with loved ones, friends, and colleagues.

5. Self-Reflection and Growth: Gratitude journaling encourages self-reflection and introspection. It allows you to recognize personal growth, appreciate your strengths, and acknowledge the progress you have made in different areas of your life.

How to Practice Gratitude Journaling

1. Set a Regular Schedule: Dedicate a specific time each day to engage in gratitude journaling. It can be in the morning to set a positive tone for the day or in the evening to reflect on the day's blessings. Consistency is key to making gratitude journaling a habit.

2. Choose a Journal: Select a notebook or journal that resonates with you. It can be a dedicated gratitude journal or any notebook that you find appealing. Personalize it with inspiring quotes, images, or decorations to make it a special space for your gratitude practice.

3. Reflect on the Day: Begin by reflecting on the day and identifying moments, experiences, or things you are grateful for. It can be as simple as a beautiful sunrise, a kind gesture from a friend, or a small accomplishment.

4. Write in Detail: Write down your gratitude entries in detail. Describe why you are grateful for each item and how it positively impacts your life. Elaborate on the feelings and emotions associated with each moment of gratitude.

5. Be Specific and Diverse: Aim for specificity in your entries. Instead of writing "I am grateful for my family," focus on individual family members and the unique qualities or actions you appreciate. Also, strive for diversity in your gratitude entries to capture various aspects of your life.

6. Challenge Yourself: Occasionally, challenge yourself to find gratitude in challenging or difficult situations. This helps develop resilience and perspective by acknowledging the lessons or silver linings within adversity.

7. Reflect and Revisit: Regularly revisit your past gratitude entries. Reflect on the moments of gratitude you have captured and notice any

patterns or recurring themes. Use this reflection to reinforce positive thinking and appreciate the abundance in your life.

Conclusion

Gratitude journaling is a transformative practice that can elevate your well-being, mindset, and relationships. By intentionally cultivating gratitude and expressing appreciation for the blessings in your life, you can shift your focus towards positivity, increase happiness, and reduce stress. Incorporate gratitude journaling into your daily routine, and witness the profound impact it can have on your overall outlook and satisfaction with life. Embrace the power of gratitude and experience the joy of finding beauty and appreciation in even the smallest moments.

Technique 14: Expressive Writing for Emotional Release and Personal Growth

EXPRESSIVE WRITING is a therapeutic practice that involves putting your thoughts and emotions into written words. It provides a cathartic outlet for self-expression, allowing you to process and release pent-up feelings, gain insights, and foster personal growth. In this section, we explore the benefits of expressive writing and provide guidance on how to engage in this powerful practice.

The Benefits of Expressive Writing

1. Emotional Release: Expressive writing provides a safe space to release and explore your emotions. By putting your thoughts and feelings onto paper, you can release emotional tension and gain a sense of relief and liberation.

2. Self-Exploration and Insight: Writing about your experiences, thoughts, and emotions can lead to self-discovery and increased self-awareness. It allows you to delve deeper into your thoughts and gain insights into patterns, beliefs, and underlying emotions.

3. Stress Reduction: Engaging in expressive writing can help reduce stress levels. By externalizing your thoughts and concerns, you create distance between yourself and the stressors, enabling you to gain perspective and experience a sense of relief.

4. Problem Solving: Writing about challenges or dilemmas can help clarify your thoughts and find solutions. It allows you to explore different perspectives, brainstorm ideas, and gain clarity on the steps needed to overcome obstacles.

5. Healing and Emotional Well-being: Expressive writing has been associated with improved emotional well-being and mental health. It can help process trauma, cope with grief, and promote healing from emotional wounds.

How to Practice Expressive Writing

1. Find a Quiet Space: Choose a quiet and comfortable space where you can focus and feel at ease. Create an environment that promotes relaxation and introspection.

2. Set a Time Limit: Allocate a specific time for your expressive writing practice. Start with a manageable duration, such as 10 to 15 minutes, and gradually increase it as you become more comfortable with the process.

3. Write Freely and Honestly: Give yourself permission to write freely and honestly. Do not worry about grammar, punctuation, or coherence. Let your thoughts flow naturally onto the paper without self-censorship.

4. Choose a Prompt: Select a prompt or topic to guide your writing. It can be a specific event, a challenging emotion, a relationship, or any aspect of your life that you want to explore. Use the prompt as a starting point for your writing.

5. Embrace Stream of Consciousness: Engage in stream of consciousness writing, where you write continuously without pausing or editing. Allow your thoughts to flow without judgment or

self-censorship. Follow the natural flow of your mind and let your writing evolve organically.

6. Reflect and Process: After completing your writing session, take a few moments to reflect on what you have written. Notice any recurring themes, insights, or patterns that emerge. Use this reflection as an opportunity for self-understanding and personal growth.

7. Practice Self-Care: Engaging in expressive writing can evoke strong emotions. Practice self-care after each session by engaging in activities that promote relaxation, such as deep breathing, meditation, or engaging in hobbies that bring you joy.

CONCLUSION

Expressive writing is a powerful tool for emotional release, self-exploration, and personal growth. By engaging in this practice, you can tap into your inner world, process emotions, and gain valuable insights. Allow yourself the freedom to express your thoughts and feelings honestly and without judgment. Embrace the transformative power of expressive writing and embark on a journey of self-discovery, healing, and personal empowerment.

Technique 15: Emotional Release Practices for Catharsis and Emotional Well-being

EMOTIONAL RELEASE PRACTICES provide a direct and visceral way to release pent-up emotions, allowing for catharsis and emotional well-being. These practices, such as crying and screaming, offer a release valve for accumulated stress, grief, anger, or any intense emotion that needs to be expressed. In this section, we explore the benefits of emotional release practices and provide guidance on how to engage in them effectively and safely.

The Benefits of Emotional Release Practices

1. Catharsis: Emotional release practices offer a cathartic experience by allowing emotions to be expressed fully and authentically. They provide an outlet for releasing built-up tension and promoting a sense of relief and release.

2. Stress Reduction: Engaging in emotional release practices can help reduce stress levels. By allowing yourself to fully experience and express emotions, you release the physiological and psychological effects of stress, promoting relaxation and a sense of calm.

3. Emotional Well-being: Emotional release practices contribute to emotional well-being by allowing for the healthy expression of emotions. They help prevent emotional suppression and encourage emotional authenticity, fostering a sense of inner peace and balance.

4. Increased Self-awareness: Engaging in emotional release practices promotes self-awareness by connecting you with your emotions and inner experiences. It allows for a deeper understanding of your emotional landscape and can uncover underlying emotions or triggers.

5. Emotional Regulation: Regularly engaging in emotional release practices can improve emotional regulation skills. By giving yourself permission to express and process emotions, you develop a greater sense of emotional resilience and the ability to navigate challenging emotions effectively.

How to Engage in Emotional Release Practices

1. Create a Safe Space: Find a private and comfortable space where you can freely express yourself without judgment or interruption. Ensure the space is safe and conducive to the intensity of emotions that may arise.

2. Allow Yourself to Feel: Give yourself permission to feel and acknowledge the emotions that are present within you. Let go of any self-judgment or criticism, and allow the emotions to flow naturally.

3. Crying: Crying is a natural and common emotional release practice. Allow yourself to cry when you feel the need, as it can provide a sense of emotional release and relief. Find a quiet and private space where you can freely express your tears.

4. Screaming or Vocal Release: Find a secluded space, such as a forest, an empty room, or your car, where you can release your emotions through screaming or vocalization. Allow yourself to let out the pent-up energy and emotions through your voice.

5. Physical Release: Engage in physical activities that facilitate emotional release, such as punching a pillow, hitting a punching bag, or engaging in vigorous exercise. Allow your body to move freely, releasing the physical tension associated with intense emotions.

6. Journaling: Combine emotional release practices with journaling. Write about your emotions, frustrations, or any thoughts or experiences that contribute to your emotional state. Use journaling as a tool to express and process your emotions.

7. Seeking Support: If engaging in emotional release practices feels overwhelming or if you need additional support, consider reaching out to a trusted friend, family member, or mental health professional. They can provide guidance, validation, and a safe space for you to express yourself.

Conclusion

Emotional release practices offer a powerful avenue for catharsis and emotional well-being. By engaging in practices like crying, screaming, or physical release, you allow yourself to express and release intense emotions, promoting stress reduction, emotional regulation, and increased self-awareness. Remember to create a safe and supportive space for these practices and seek support when needed. Embrace the healing power of emotional release and honor your emotions as an essential part of your well-being.

Technique 16: Art Therapy and Creative Expression for Emotional Release and Self-Exploration

ART THERAPY AND CREATIVE expression provide a unique and powerful way to process emotions, promote self-exploration, and enhance overall well-being. Through various artistic mediums, individuals can tap into their inner creativity and use art as a means of communication and emotional release. In this section, we explore the benefits of art therapy and creative expression and provide guidance on how to engage in these practices for emotional well-being.

The Benefits of Art Therapy and Creative Expression

1. Emotional Release: Art therapy and creative expression offer a non-verbal outlet for expressing and releasing emotions. Engaging in artistic activities allows emotions to be externalized and transformed into visual or tactile forms, facilitating emotional release and catharsis.

2. Self-Exploration and Insight: Creating art provides a unique opportunity for self-exploration and gaining insights into one's emotions, thoughts, and inner world. The process of engaging with art materials and expressing oneself visually can uncover subconscious emotions, beliefs, and patterns, leading to greater self-awareness.

3. Stress Reduction: Immersing oneself in art-making can promote relaxation and stress reduction. The focus required during the creative process can divert attention from stressors, providing a calming and meditative experience. Engaging in art also stimulates the production of endorphins, enhancing mood and reducing stress.

4. Communication and Expression: For individuals who find it challenging to verbalize their emotions, art therapy and creative expression offer alternative means of communication. Art becomes a

language through which thoughts, feelings, and experiences can be expressed, shared, and understood by others.

5. Personal Growth and Empowerment: Engaging in art therapy and creative expression can foster personal growth and empowerment. It allows individuals to express their unique perspectives, cultivate self-acceptance, and develop a sense of agency and control over their creative process.

How to Engage in Art Therapy and Creative Expression

1. Choose an Artistic Medium: Select an artistic medium that resonates with you, such as painting, drawing, sculpting, collage, or any other form of creative expression. Consider the medium that feels most comfortable or intriguing to you.

2. Create a Supportive Environment: Set up a dedicated space for your art therapy practice. Make it a comfortable and inspiring environment that encourages creativity and self-expression. Gather art supplies and materials that align with your chosen medium.

3. Engage in Free Expression: Allow yourself to freely express without judgment or expectation. Let go of self-criticism and perfectionism, and embrace the process of exploration and experimentation. Focus on the experience rather than the final outcome.

4. Follow Your Intuition: Allow your intuition to guide your artistic process. Trust your instincts and let your inner creativity flow. Let go of preconceived notions and embrace the spontaneity and freedom that artistic expression offers.

5. Reflect on Your Artwork: Take time to reflect on your artwork after completing a session. Observe the colors, shapes, and symbols present and consider the emotions or messages conveyed. Journal about your experience and insights gained through the creative process.

6. Seek Professional Guidance: If you desire additional support or want to delve deeper into art therapy, consider seeking guidance from a certified art therapist. They can provide expert assistance in navigating

the artistic process and help you explore emotions and themes in a therapeutic manner.

Conclusion

Art therapy and creative expression offer a transformative and enriching experience for emotional release, self-exploration, and personal growth. Through the use of artistic mediums, individuals can express and process emotions, gain insights into their inner world, and foster overall well-being. Embrace the power of art as a tool for communication, self-expression, and healing. Engage in art therapy and creative expression, and allow the process to guide you on a journey of self-discovery, emotional release, and empowerment.

Chapter 5: Healthy Lifestyle Habits for Stress Reduction and Overall Well-being

Maintaining a healthy lifestyle is crucial for managing stress and promoting overall well-being. By incorporating healthy habits into your daily routine, you can effectively reduce stress levels, enhance resilience, and improve your physical and mental health. In this section, we explore various lifestyle habits that contribute to stress reduction and provide guidance on how to integrate them into your life.

Technique 17: Proper Sleep Hygiene for Restful Nights and Reduced Stress

GOOD SLEEP HYGIENE practices are essential for promoting restful nights and reducing stress levels. By adopting healthy sleep habits and creating a sleep-friendly environment, you can improve the quality and duration of your sleep, leading to enhanced well-being and better stress management. In this section, we delve into the principles of proper sleep hygiene and provide practical tips to help you establish a soothing sleep routine.

Understanding Sleep Hygiene

1. Maintain a Consistent Sleep Schedule: Go to bed and wake up at the same time every day, even on weekends. Consistency helps regulate your body's internal clock, optimizing sleep quality and promoting a more natural sleep-wake cycle.

2. Create a Relaxing Bedtime Routine: Establish a pre-sleep routine that signals to your body that it's time to wind down. Engage in relaxing activities such as reading a book, taking a warm bath,

practicing gentle stretches, or listening to calming music. Avoid stimulating activities or electronics close to bedtime.

3. Create a Sleep-Friendly Environment: Make your bedroom a peaceful and comfortable sanctuary dedicated to sleep. Keep the room cool, dark, and quiet, using curtains or blinds to block out excess light and earplugs or white noise machines to minimize disruptive sounds.

4. Invest in a Quality Mattress and Pillows: Choose a supportive mattress and pillows that suit your comfort preferences. A comfortable sleep surface promotes better sleep posture, reduces discomfort, and enhances sleep quality.

5. Limit Exposure to Blue Light: Reduce exposure to blue light emitted by electronic devices, such as smartphones, tablets, and computers, in the evening. Blue light can interfere with your natural sleep-wake cycle. Use blue light filters or switch to "night mode" on electronic devices to minimize exposure.

6. Avoid Stimulants and Heavy Meals: Limit or avoid consuming stimulants like caffeine and nicotine, especially in the evening. These substances can disrupt sleep patterns and make it harder to fall asleep. Additionally, avoid heavy meals close to bedtime, as digestion can interfere with sleep quality.

7. Create a Relaxing Bedroom Environment: Make your bedroom a calming and clutter-free space. Use soft, comfortable bedding, and consider incorporating relaxation elements like essential oils, lavender sachets, or gentle lighting to create a soothing ambiance.

8. Exercise Regularly: Engage in regular physical activity, but avoid intense exercise close to bedtime. Regular exercise promotes better sleep quality and reduces stress levels. However, allow sufficient time between exercise and bedtime to allow your body to wind down.

9. Manage Stress and Anxiety: Implement stress management techniques, such as relaxation exercises, meditation, or journaling, to reduce stress and anxiety before bedtime. Clear your mind and create a sense of calm to prepare for a restful sleep.

10. Limit Napping: If you have trouble sleeping at night, limit daytime napping or keep it short (around 20-30 minutes) and avoid napping too close to bedtime. Long or late-day naps can interfere with your sleep schedule.

Conclusion

By prioritizing proper sleep hygiene, you can create an optimal sleep environment and establish healthy bedtime routines. Restful nights of sleep are crucial for reducing stress levels, enhancing overall well-being, and equipping you with the resilience to face the challenges of each day. Incorporate these sleep hygiene practices into your life, and enjoy the rejuvenating benefits of restorative sleep.

Technique 18: Balanced Nutrition and Hydration for Stress Reduction and Vitality

PROPER NUTRITION AND hydration play a significant role in stress reduction and maintaining overall vitality. Fueling your body with nutritious foods and staying adequately hydrated not only supports physical health but also has a profound impact on your mental and emotional well-being. In this section, we explore the importance of balanced nutrition and hydration in stress management and provide practical tips for incorporating healthy eating habits into your lifestyle.

Understanding Balanced Nutrition

1. Eat a Variety of Nutrient-Dense Foods: Include a wide range of fruits, vegetables, whole grains, lean proteins, and healthy fats in your diet. These nutrient-dense foods provide essential vitamins, minerals, antioxidants, and fiber that support overall health and help combat stress.

2. Focus on Whole Foods: Prioritize whole, unprocessed foods over processed and refined options. Whole foods retain their natural nutrients and offer more significant benefits for your body and mind.

Choose fresh fruits and vegetables, whole grains, legumes, nuts, and seeds.

3. Mindful Eating: Practice mindful eating by paying attention to your body's hunger and fullness cues. Slow down, savor each bite, and be present during meals. This helps you make healthier food choices, enhances digestion, and promotes a sense of satisfaction.

4. Balance Macronutrients: Aim for a balance of carbohydrates, proteins, and fats in your meals. Carbohydrates provide energy, proteins support muscle repair and growth, and healthy fats aid in nutrient absorption and support brain health.

5. Hydration is Key: Stay hydrated by drinking an adequate amount of water throughout the day. Dehydration can contribute to increased stress levels and fatigue. Carry a reusable water bottle with you to remind yourself to drink water regularly.

6. Limit Added Sugars and Processed Foods: Minimize your intake of added sugars, sugary beverages, and processed foods. These can cause blood sugar spikes and crashes, leading to increased stress and fatigue. Opt for natural sweeteners and choose whole, unprocessed alternatives.

7. Be Mindful of Caffeine and Alcohol Intake: Limit your consumption of caffeine and alcohol, as they can impact your sleep quality, energy levels, and stress response. Monitor your intake and consider alternatives like herbal teas or infused water for hydration.

8. Plan and Prepare Meals: Plan your meals in advance and prepare them at home as much as possible. This allows you to have more control over the ingredients and portion sizes. Use meal prepping techniques to save time and ensure healthier choices throughout the week.

9. Listen to Your Body: Tune in to your body's signals and honor its needs. Eat when you're hungry, and stop when you're comfortably full. Pay attention to how different foods make you feel and adjust your choices accordingly.

10. Seek Professional Guidance: If you have specific dietary concerns or need personalized advice, consider consulting with a

registered dietitian or nutritionist who can provide tailored guidance and support.

Conclusion

By adopting a balanced approach to nutrition and hydration, you can support your body and mind in managing stress and maintaining vitality. Nourish yourself with whole, nutrient-dense foods, stay hydrated, and listen to your body's cues. Making conscious choices about what you eat and drink can have a profound impact on your overall well-being and provide you with the energy and resilience to navigate life's challenges with ease.

Technique 19: Stress-Relieving Herbs and Supplements for Enhanced Well-being

HERBS AND SUPPLEMENTS have long been used to support stress reduction and promote overall well-being. While they are not a substitute for a healthy lifestyle and professional medical advice, certain herbs and supplements have shown potential in helping to manage stress levels and improve resilience. In this section, we explore some commonly used stress-relieving herbs and supplements and provide insights on their potential benefits and considerations.

Understanding Stress-Relieving Herbs and Supplements

1. Ashwagandha: Ashwagandha is an adaptogenic herb known for its stress-reducing properties. It helps regulate the body's stress response, supports a sense of calm, and promotes overall well-being. Considered safe for most individuals, ashwagandha is available in capsule, powder, or liquid form.

2. Rhodiola Rosea: Rhodiola rosea is another adaptogenic herb that may help reduce stress and enhance mental performance. It has been traditionally used to combat fatigue, improve mood, and increase resilience. Consult with a healthcare professional for appropriate dosing and guidance.

3. Lavender: Lavender is a fragrant herb known for its calming and soothing effects. Its aroma has been shown to reduce anxiety and promote relaxation. Lavender can be used in essential oil form for aromatherapy, incorporated into teas, or used in bath products for a calming experience.

4. Chamomile: Chamomile is a gentle herb often used for its calming properties. It can help alleviate stress, anxiety, and promote better sleep. Enjoy chamomile tea before bedtime or as a soothing beverage throughout the day.

5. Magnesium: Magnesium is a mineral that plays a vital role in stress management and relaxation. It supports healthy nerve and muscle function and helps regulate stress hormones. Consider magnesium supplements or incorporate magnesium-rich foods like leafy greens, nuts, seeds, and whole grains into your diet.

6. Omega-3 Fatty Acids: Omega-3 fatty acids, found in fatty fish, walnuts, flaxseeds, and chia seeds, have been linked to improved mood and reduced inflammation. Consider incorporating omega-3 supplements or consuming these foods regularly to support overall well-being.

7. Vitamin B Complex: B vitamins, particularly B6, B9 (folate), and B12, are involved in the production of neurotransmitters that regulate mood and stress response. Consider a vitamin B complex supplement or consume foods rich in B vitamins such as leafy greens, legumes, and fortified cereals.

8. Passionflower: Passionflower is an herb known for its calming properties. It may help reduce anxiety, promote relaxation, and improve sleep quality. Passionflower can be consumed as a tea or in supplement form.

9. Valerian Root: Valerian root is a herb commonly used for its calming and sleep-promoting effects. It may help reduce anxiety and improve sleep quality. Valerian root is available in capsule or tincture form.

10. Consult with a Healthcare Professional: Before starting any herbal supplements, it is essential to consult with a healthcare professional, especially if you have any pre-existing medical conditions, take medications, or are pregnant or breastfeeding.

Conclusion

Stress-relieving herbs and supplements can be valuable tools in your stress management toolkit. While individual responses may vary, incorporating these natural remedies into a healthy lifestyle may help support your well-being and enhance resilience. However, it is important to remember that herbs and supplements are not a replacement for professional medical advice, and it is always advisable to consult with a healthcare professional before starting any new regimen. Explore these options, listen to your body, and find the best approach that works for you in reducing stress and promoting a sense of calm.

Technique 20: Relaxation Techniques for Stress Reduction and Deep Relaxation

RELAXATION TECHNIQUES are valuable tools for managing stress, promoting relaxation, and restoring a sense of calm. By incorporating specific relaxation practices into your daily routine, you can activate your body's relaxation response, reduce muscle tension, and cultivate a state of deep relaxation. In this section, we explore various relaxation techniques, including progressive muscle relaxation, and provide guidance on how to incorporate them into your stress management regimen.

Understanding Relaxation Techniques

1. Progressive Muscle Relaxation (PMR): PMR is a relaxation technique that involves systematically tensing and relaxing different muscle groups. By deliberately tensing and releasing tension, you can

promote relaxation, alleviate muscle tension, and reduce stress levels. Practice PMR by following these steps:

- Find a quiet and comfortable space where you can sit or lie down.
- Start by focusing on your breath, taking slow, deep breaths to calm your mind.
- Begin with one muscle group, such as your hands or arms. Tense the muscles in that area for a few seconds, then release and let them fully relax.
- Move on to the next muscle group, progressively working your way through your body, tensing and releasing each muscle group.
- Pay attention to the sensations of tension and relaxation as you go, and take your time to fully relax each muscle group.
- Finish by taking a few moments to enjoy the overall feeling of relaxation in your body.

2. Deep Breathing Exercises: Deep breathing exercises are simple yet powerful techniques for activating the body's relaxation response and reducing stress. Practice deep breathing by following these steps:

- Find a comfortable position, either sitting or lying down.
- Place one hand on your abdomen and the other on your chest.
- Take a slow, deep breath in through your nose, allowing your abdomen to rise and expand as you fill your lungs with air.
- Exhale slowly through your mouth, emptying your lungs completely and allowing your abdomen to fall.
- Continue this deep breathing pattern, focusing on the sensation of your breath and allowing your body to relax with each breath.

3. Guided Imagery: Guided imagery is a relaxation technique that involves visualizing calming and peaceful scenes or scenarios. It can help redirect your attention away from stress and promote a sense of relaxation. Practice guided imagery by following these steps:

- Find a quiet and comfortable space where you can relax without distractions.

- Close your eyes and take a few deep breaths to relax your body and mind.
- Choose a calming scene or scenario in your mind, such as a beach, a forest, or a peaceful garden.
- Visualize the details of this scene, engaging your senses to imagine the sights, sounds, smells, and sensations associated with it.
- Spend a few minutes fully immersing yourself in this imaginary scene, allowing yourself to experience a sense of tranquility and peace.

4. Meditation: Meditation is a practice that involves training the mind to focus and redirect thoughts, ultimately promoting a sense of calm and mental clarity. There are various meditation techniques to explore, including mindfulness meditation, loving-kindness meditation, and breath awareness meditation. Find a meditation style that resonates with you and incorporate regular meditation sessions into your routine.

5. Yoga and Stretching: Yoga and stretching exercises combine physical movement with deep breathing and mindfulness, making them effective relaxation techniques. Engaging in gentle yoga poses or stretching routines can help release muscle tension, improve flexibility, and cultivate a sense of relaxation and well-being. Consider attending yoga classes or following online tutorials to learn proper techniques and sequences.

6. Massage and Bodywork: Massage and bodywork therapies, such as Swedish massage, deep tissue massage, or reflexology, can provide physical and emotional relaxation by relieving muscle tension, improving circulation, and reducing stress hormones. Schedule regular sessions with a professional therapist or learn self-massage techniques for relaxation at home.

Conclusion

Incorporating relaxation techniques into your daily routine can be transformative for managing stress and promoting deep relaxation. Whether you choose progressive muscle relaxation, deep breathing exercises, guided imagery, meditation, yoga, or massage, these practices can help you activate your body's relaxation response, reduce muscle tension, and cultivate a state of calm. Experiment with different techniques, find what resonates with you, and make relaxation a priority in your stress management journey. Remember to practice regularly and be patient with yourself as you develop these skills. With consistent effort and commitment, you can find solace in the midst of life's stresses and enjoy the many benefits of deep relaxation.

Chapter 6: Cognitive Strategies for Stress Management and Positive Thinking

Cognitive strategies are powerful tools for managing stress by shifting your mindset, reframing negative thoughts, and cultivating a positive outlook. By becoming aware of your thoughts and beliefs, you can challenge and replace unhelpful thinking patterns that contribute to stress and adopt healthier perspectives. In this section, we explore various cognitive strategies that can support your stress management journey and promote a more optimistic and resilient mindset.

Understanding Cognitive Strategies

1. Thought Awareness: The first step in cognitive strategies is becoming aware of your thoughts. Pay attention to the stream of thoughts running through your mind and notice any recurring patterns or negative self-talk. Awareness allows you to identify stress-inducing thoughts and examine their accuracy and impact on your well-being.

2. Cognitive Restructuring: Cognitive restructuring involves challenging and replacing negative or distorted thoughts with more realistic and positive ones. Practice these steps to reframe your thinking:

- Identify a stressful thought or belief that causes distress.
- Examine the evidence for and against the thought. Is it based on facts or assumptions?
- Challenge irrational or exaggerated thoughts by considering alternative explanations or perspectives.
- Replace negative thoughts with more balanced and positive ones.

- Practice affirmations or positive self-talk to reinforce the new thought patterns.

3. Reframing: Reframing involves shifting your perspective on a situation to see it in a more positive or constructive light. It involves consciously choosing to focus on the positive aspects or potential opportunities rather than dwelling on the negative. Reframing helps you reframe challenges as opportunities for growth and resilience.

4. Gratitude Practice: Cultivating an attitude of gratitude is a powerful cognitive strategy for stress management. Regularly practicing gratitude can shift your focus from stress and negativity to appreciation and positivity. Keep a gratitude journal, write down three things you are grateful for each day, or simply take a few moments each day to reflect on the blessings in your life.

5. Positive Self-Talk: Pay attention to your internal dialogue and replace self-criticism or negative self-talk with positive and empowering statements. Use affirmations, such as "I am capable," "I can handle challenges," or "I am resilient," to reinforce positive beliefs about yourself and your ability to navigate stress.

6. Mindfulness and Acceptance: Mindfulness involves being fully present in the moment without judgment. By practicing mindfulness, you can observe your thoughts and emotions without getting caught up in them. This allows you to respond to stressors with greater clarity and calmness. Acceptance is an essential aspect of mindfulness, acknowledging that some things are beyond your control and letting go of the need to control everything.

7. Problem-Solving: Engaging in problem-solving strategies can help you feel more empowered and in control when faced with stressful situations. Break down problems into manageable steps, brainstorm potential solutions, and take action. By focusing on solutions rather than dwelling on problems, you can reduce stress and work towards positive outcomes.

8. Social Support: Seeking social support and connecting with others can provide a valuable cognitive boost during stressful times. Share your thoughts and concerns with trusted friends or family members, seek guidance from a mentor or therapist, or participate in support groups. Sharing your experiences and receiving support can provide new perspectives and alleviate stress.

Conclusion

Cognitive strategies offer powerful tools for managing stress and promoting positive thinking. By becoming aware of your thoughts, challenging negative thinking patterns, reframing perspectives, practicing gratitude, and cultivating mindfulness, you can cultivate a more resilient mindset and navigate stress with greater ease. Remember that cognitive strategies require practice and patience, but the effort is well worth the positive impact on your overall well-being. Incorporate these strategies into your daily life, and over time, you'll develop a more optimistic and empowered approach to stress management.

Technique 21: Cognitive Restructuring: Transforming Negative Thinking Patterns

COGNITIVE RESTRUCTURING is a powerful technique that allows you to identify and challenge negative or unhelpful thoughts, beliefs, and assumptions. By restructuring your thinking, you can replace negative patterns with more balanced and positive thoughts, leading to reduced stress and improved well-being. In this section, we explore the process of cognitive restructuring and provide practical strategies for transforming negative thinking patterns.

Understanding Cognitive Restructuring

1. Identify Negative Thoughts: The first step in cognitive restructuring is to become aware of your negative thoughts. Pay attention to the thoughts that arise when you're feeling stressed or

overwhelmed. Notice any recurring patterns or distorted thinking that contributes to your stress.

2. Question the Accuracy of Negative Thoughts: Once you've identified negative thoughts, challenge their accuracy. Ask yourself if there is evidence to support these thoughts or if they are based on assumptions or biases. Often, negative thoughts are not grounded in reality and can be distorted by our own perceptions.

3. Examine Alternative Explanations: Explore alternative explanations or perspectives for the situations that trigger negative thoughts. Consider other possible interpretations or factors that may contribute to the situation. This helps broaden your perspective and introduces more balanced thinking.

4. Replace Negative Thoughts with Positive and Realistic Ones: After challenging the accuracy of negative thoughts, replace them with positive and realistic alternatives. Choose thoughts that are more aligned with the evidence and consider the possibilities for more positive outcomes. For example, if you have a negative thought like "I always mess things up," replace it with "I am capable of learning from my mistakes and improving."

5. Practice Affirmations: Affirmations are positive statements that you repeat to yourself to reinforce new thought patterns. Choose affirmations that counteract the negative thoughts and beliefs you want to change. Repeat them regularly, especially when you notice negative thinking patterns resurfacing.

6. Monitor and Challenge Cognitive Distortions: Cognitive distortions are common thinking errors that contribute to negative thoughts. By becoming aware of these distortions, you can challenge and replace them with more accurate and balanced thoughts. Some common cognitive distortions include:

- All-or-Nothing Thinking: Seeing things in black-and-white terms without considering the shades of gray.

- Overgeneralization: Drawing sweeping conclusions based on a single event or experience.
- Catastrophizing: Magnifying the importance or potential negative outcomes of a situation.
- Personalization: Assuming responsibility for things that are beyond your control.
- Mind Reading: Believing that you know what others are thinking or that they have negative intentions.

7. Keep a Thought Journal: Keep a journal to record your negative thoughts and their associated emotions. This helps you identify patterns and triggers, allowing you to challenge and restructure those thoughts effectively. Write down the negative thought, the situation that triggered it, any evidence supporting or refuting the thought, and a more balanced and realistic thought to replace it.

8. Seek Support: Changing negative thinking patterns can be challenging, so seek support from trusted friends, family members, or a mental health professional. They can provide encouragement, guidance, and different perspectives that aid in the cognitive restructuring process.

Conclusion

Cognitive restructuring is a powerful technique for transforming negative thinking patterns and reducing stress. By becoming aware of your negative thoughts, questioning their accuracy, examining alternative explanations, and replacing them with positive and realistic thoughts, you can cultivate a more balanced and resilient mindset. Remember that cognitive restructuring takes practice and patience. With consistent effort, you can develop the ability to reframe your thoughts and approach stressful situations with greater clarity, resilience, and well-being.

Technique 22: Reframing and Perspective Shifting: Harnessing the Power of Positive

Thinking

REFRAMING AND PERSPECTIVE shifting are powerful cognitive strategies that allow you to change how you perceive and interpret stressful situations. By consciously choosing to focus on the positive aspects or potential opportunities, you can transform your perspective and reduce stress. In this section, we explore the art of reframing and provide practical techniques for shifting your perspective to cultivate a more positive and resilient mindset.

Understanding Reframing and Perspective Shifting

1. Recognize Negative Thought Patterns: The first step in reframing and perspective shifting is to become aware of negative thought patterns. Notice when you engage in negative self-talk or when you automatically perceive situations in a negative light. Recognize that your initial interpretation may not be the only way to view the situation.

2. Challenge Negative Assumptions: Once you've identified negative thought patterns, challenge the assumptions that underlie them. Ask yourself if there are alternative explanations or perspectives that may be equally valid. Consider the possibility that your initial interpretation may be influenced by biases or limited information.

3. Find the Silver Lining: Look for the silver lining in challenging situations. Ask yourself what positive aspects or opportunities may arise from the circumstances. For example, if faced with a setback at work, you could reframe it as a learning opportunity or a chance to develop resilience.

4. Practice Gratitude: Cultivating gratitude can shift your focus from stress and negativity to appreciation and positivity. Take time each day to reflect on things you are grateful for, both big and small. This practice helps reframe your perspective by acknowledging the positive aspects of your life.

5. Seek Alternative Explanations: Explore different interpretations or explanations for the situations that trigger negative thoughts.

Consider other people's perspectives and try to see the situation from their point of view. This broadens your understanding and opens the door to new possibilities.

6. Empathy and Compassion: Practice empathy and compassion towards yourself and others. By understanding that everyone has their own struggles and challenges, you can develop a more compassionate perspective. This helps you reframe situations by considering the motivations and emotions of others involved.

7. Visualize Positive Outcomes: Use visualization techniques to imagine positive outcomes or successful resolutions to stressful situations. Visualizing positive scenarios helps shift your perspective from a fear-based mindset to a more optimistic one. This can increase your confidence and reduce stress.

8. Practice Self-Reflection: Engage in regular self-reflection to gain insight into your patterns of thinking and how they impact your perception of stressful events. This self-awareness allows you to consciously choose alternative perspectives and reframe situations more effectively.

9. Surround Yourself with Positive Influences: Surround yourself with people who have a positive outlook on life. Their optimistic perspectives can be contagious and help you shift your own mindset. Engage in activities that inspire and uplift you, such as reading inspiring books or listening to motivational podcasts.

Conclusion

Reframing and perspective shifting are powerful cognitive strategies that allow you to cultivate a more positive and resilient mindset. By challenging negative assumptions, finding the silver lining, practicing gratitude, seeking alternative explanations, and visualizing positive outcomes, you can reframe stressful situations and reduce their impact on your well-being. Remember that reframing takes practice and effort, but with time, it becomes a natural and empowering way of navigating life's challenges. Embrace the power of positive thinking, and you'll discover new perspectives that lead to greater resilience, happiness, and stress management.

Technique 23: Positive Affirmations and Self-Talk: Harnessing the Power of Positive Words

POSITIVE AFFIRMATIONS and self-talk are powerful tools for managing stress and cultivating a positive mindset. By consciously choosing uplifting and empowering words, you can reshape your thoughts, beliefs, and emotions. In this section, we explore the benefits of positive affirmations and self-talk and provide practical techniques for incorporating them into your daily life.

Understanding Positive Affirmations

1. What Are Affirmations? Affirmations are positive statements that you repeat to yourself to reinforce desired thoughts and beliefs. They are designed to challenge and replace negative or self-limiting beliefs with empowering and uplifting thoughts. Affirmations can be used to boost confidence, reduce stress, and cultivate a positive mindset.

2. Crafting Effective Affirmations: When creating affirmations, ensure they are specific, meaningful, and in the present tense. Use positive language and focus on what you want to achieve or experience. For example, instead of saying "I am not stressed," say "I am calm and at peace."

3. Repeating Affirmations: Repeat your affirmations regularly, ideally in the morning or before bed. Say them with conviction and belief, visualizing the positive outcomes you desire. Repetition helps to reinforce new neural pathways and overwrite negative thought patterns with positive ones.

4. Affirmations for Stress Management: Create affirmations specifically tailored to managing stress. Examples include "I handle

stressful situations with ease and grace," "I am resilient and bounce back from challenges," or "I embrace relaxation and take time for self-care."

5. Affirmations for Self-Confidence: Boost your self-confidence by using affirmations such as "I believe in my abilities," "I am worthy of success and happiness," or "I am confident in who I am."

Understanding Self-Talk

1. The Power of Self-Talk: Self-talk refers to the internal dialogue we have with ourselves throughout the day. It shapes our beliefs, emotions, and actions. By becoming aware of our self-talk and intentionally choosing positive and supportive language, we can significantly impact our stress levels and overall well-being.

2. Identify Negative Self-Talk: Pay attention to your internal dialogue and identify any negative or self-defeating statements. Notice when you engage in self-criticism, self-doubt, or negative predictions about the future. Awareness is the first step in transforming negative self-talk.

3. Challenge Negative Self-Talk: Once you recognize negative self-talk, challenge its validity. Ask yourself if there is evidence to support these negative beliefs or if they are simply self-imposed limitations. Challenge negative statements with counterarguments that highlight your strengths and past successes.

4. Replace Negative with Positive Self-Talk: Replace negative self-talk with positive and supportive statements. Encourage yourself, acknowledge your efforts, and remind yourself of your capabilities. For example, replace "I always mess up" with "I am learning and growing with every experience."

5. Practice Self-Compassion: Be kind and compassionate toward yourself in your self-talk. Treat yourself as you would a supportive friend, offering words of understanding and encouragement. Use phrases like "I am doing the best I can," "It's okay to make mistakes," and "I deserve love and kindness."

Incorporating Positive Affirmations and Self-Talk in Daily Life

1. Morning Affirmation Ritual: Start your day with a few minutes of positive affirmations. Repeat affirmations that resonate with you, visualizing the positive outcomes you desire. This sets a positive tone for the day ahead.

2. Mirror Affirmations: Stand in front of a mirror and recite affirmations while looking into your own eyes. This practice enhances the emotional impact of the affirmations and strengthens your connection with yourself.

3. Sticky Note Reminders: Place sticky notes with affirmations in visible locations, such as your desk, bathroom mirror, or refrigerator. These reminders reinforce positive self-talk throughout the day.

4. Pause and Reset: When you catch yourself engaging in negative self-talk or feeling stressed, pause and take a deep breath. Replace the negative thoughts with positive affirmations or comforting self-talk. Remind yourself that you have the power to choose your thoughts and emotions.

Conclusion

Positive affirmations and self-talk are transformative techniques for managing stress and fostering a positive mindset. By crafting effective affirmations, repeating them consistently, challenging negative self-talk, and replacing it with positive and supportive language, you can reshape your thoughts and beliefs. Incorporate these practices into your daily life and witness the profound impact they have on your stress levels, self-confidence, and overall well-being. Embrace the power of positive words and empower yourself to navigate life's challenges with resilience and optimism.

Technique 24: Problem-Solving Techniques: Empowering Solutions for Stressful Situations

WHEN FACED WITH STRESS and challenges, having effective problem-solving techniques can help you approach difficulties with clarity and confidence. This section explores various problem-solving strategies that empower you to tackle stressful situations head-on and find practical solutions. By developing your problem-solving skills, you can navigate obstacles with resilience and minimize the impact of stress on your well-being.

Understanding Problem-Solving

1. Define the Problem: The first step in problem-solving is clearly defining the issue at hand. Take time to identify and understand the specific problem you are facing. Break it down into smaller components if necessary to gain a comprehensive understanding.

2. Generate Alternative Solutions: Brainstorm a list of potential solutions to the problem. Be open-minded and creative, considering a range of options without judgment. Encourage yourself to think outside the box and explore unconventional approaches.

3. Evaluate and Select Solutions: Assess the potential pros and cons of each solution. Consider factors such as feasibility, practicality, and potential outcomes. Select the solution that aligns best with your values, resources, and desired outcomes.

4. Implement the Solution: Once you have chosen a solution, develop an action plan and begin implementing it. Break the plan down into smaller steps and set achievable milestones to track your progress. Take proactive steps to put the solution into action.

5. Monitor and Evaluate: Continuously monitor the effectiveness of the implemented solution. Assess whether it is achieving the desired outcomes and if any adjustments are necessary. Be willing to adapt and make changes as needed.

6. Learn from Experience: Reflect on the problem-solving process and learn from your experiences. Take note of what worked well and what could be improved for future problem-solving situations. Use each challenge as an opportunity for growth and personal development.

Problem-Solving Techniques for Stress Management

1. The Five W's Technique: Use the Five W's (Who, What, When, Where, Why) to thoroughly examine the problem and gain a comprehensive understanding of its root causes. This technique helps you identify the underlying factors contributing to the stress and guides your problem-solving efforts.

2. SWOT Analysis: Conduct a SWOT (Strengths, Weaknesses, Opportunities, Threats) analysis to assess the situation objectively. Identify your strengths and weaknesses, as well as potential opportunities and threats. This analysis helps you leverage your strengths and address weaknesses to develop effective solutions.

3. Mind Mapping: Create a visual mind map to visually represent the problem and explore potential solutions. Start with the central problem and branch out with various subtopics and potential solutions. Mind mapping allows you to see connections and possibilities that may not be apparent initially.

4. Role-Playing: Engage in role-playing exercises to gain different perspectives on the problem. Enlist the help of a trusted friend or colleague and take turns assuming different roles in the situation. This technique allows you to consider alternative viewpoints and generate creative solutions.

5. Seek Input from Others: Don't hesitate to seek input and advice from others. Consult with trusted friends, mentors, or professionals who may have insights or experiences relevant to the problem. Their perspectives can provide valuable guidance and broaden your problem-solving options.

6. Break the Problem Down: If the problem seems overwhelming, break it down into smaller, manageable parts. Address each component individually and develop solutions for each part. This approach helps you tackle complex problems systematically and reduces stress by focusing on achievable tasks.

Conclusion

Effective problem-solving techniques are essential tools for managing stress and overcoming obstacles. By defining the problem, generating alternative solutions, evaluating and selecting the best approach, implementing the solution, monitoring progress, and learning from the experience, you can navigate stressful situations with confidence and resilience. Incorporate problem-solving strategies into your stress management toolkit, and empower yourself to confront challenges head-on. With a proactive problem-solving mindset, you can transform stress into opportunities for growth and success.

Chapter 7: Social Support and Connection: Building a Strong Support Network for Stress Resilience

Social support and connection play a vital role in managing stress and promoting overall well-being. Building meaningful relationships and having a strong support network can provide comfort, encouragement, and practical assistance during challenging times. In this section, we explore the importance of social support, ways to cultivate meaningful connections, and strategies for seeking and nurturing relationships that contribute to stress resilience.

Technique 25: Nurturing Healthy Relationships: Building Strong Bonds for Stress Resilience

NURTURING HEALTHY RELATIONSHIPS is essential for managing stress and fostering overall well-being. Strong and supportive relationships provide a sense of belonging, emotional comfort, and practical assistance during challenging times. In this section, we explore strategies for cultivating and maintaining healthy relationships that contribute to stress resilience and enhance our overall quality of life.

Understanding Healthy Relationships

1. Mutual Respect: Healthy relationships are built on mutual respect and appreciation for one another. Each person's thoughts, feelings, and boundaries are acknowledged and valued. Respectful communication and behavior create a safe and nurturing environment for both individuals.

2. Effective Communication: Open and honest communication is key to nurturing healthy relationships. It involves active listening, expressing oneself clearly and respectfully, and being open to understanding different perspectives. Effective communication fosters understanding, reduces misunderstandings, and strengthens the bond between individuals.

3. Trust and Honesty: Trust is the foundation of healthy relationships. It involves being reliable, keeping commitments, and maintaining confidentiality. Honesty and transparency build trust, allowing individuals to feel secure and supported in their relationships.

4. Emotional Support: Healthy relationships provide emotional support during times of stress or difficulty. This involves being empathetic, validating feelings, and offering comfort and encouragement. Emotional support creates a sense of safety and reassurance, enabling individuals to navigate stress more effectively.

Strategies for Nurturing Healthy Relationships

1. Quality Time: Dedicate quality time to spend with your loved ones. Create opportunities for meaningful connections by engaging in activities together, having regular conversations, or simply enjoying each other's company. Quality time strengthens bonds and deepens the emotional connection between individuals.

2. Active Listening: Practice active listening in your relationships. Give your full attention to the other person, listen without judgment, and show genuine interest in their thoughts and feelings. Reflect back what you've heard to ensure understanding and validation. Active listening fosters deeper connections and enhances communication.

3. Express Appreciation: Regularly express your appreciation for the people in your life. Acknowledge their contributions, qualities, and efforts. Expressing gratitude and appreciation strengthens the bond between individuals and reinforces positive feelings within the relationship.

4. Healthy Conflict Resolution: Conflict is a natural part of any relationship. Learn and practice healthy conflict resolution skills, such as active problem-solving, compromise, and empathy. Address conflicts with respect and openness, seeking solutions that consider the needs and perspectives of all parties involved.

5. Boundaries and Self-Care: Establish and respect personal boundaries within your relationships. Communicate your needs, limits, and preferences clearly and assertively. Encourage others to do the same. Prioritize self-care and encourage your loved ones to prioritize their well-being as well. Respecting boundaries promotes healthier and more balanced relationships.

6. Foster Growth and Support Goals: Encourage personal growth and support the goals of your loved ones. Celebrate their achievements, offer encouragement during challenges, and provide assistance when needed. Supporting each other's growth cultivates a positive and uplifting environment within the relationship.

Conclusion

Nurturing healthy relationships is an essential aspect of managing stress and promoting overall well-being. By cultivating mutual respect, effective communication, trust, and emotional support, we create a strong foundation for meaningful connections. Investing time and effort into nurturing our relationships allows us to build resilience, find comfort during stressful times, and experience the profound benefits of supportive bonds.

Technique 26: Seeking Emotional Support: Building a Strong Support Network for Stress Resilience

SEEKING EMOTIONAL SUPPORT is a crucial aspect of managing stress and promoting emotional well-being. Having a strong support network can provide comfort, validation, and guidance during challenging times. In this section, we explore strategies for seeking and cultivating emotional support, allowing you to build a network of individuals who can offer understanding, empathy, and a safe space for emotional expression.

The Importance of Emotional Support

1. Understanding Emotional Support: Emotional support involves seeking understanding, empathy, and validation from others. It provides a safe space to express emotions, share experiences, and receive comfort and encouragement. Emotional support plays a pivotal role in managing stress, promoting emotional well-being, and enhancing resilience.

2. Validation and Empathy: Seeking emotional support allows us to feel validated and understood. When we share our feelings and experiences with empathetic individuals, it helps us realize that we are not alone in our struggles. Validation and empathy contribute to a sense of belonging and reduce feelings of isolation.

3. Perspective and Guidance: Emotional support from trusted individuals can offer fresh perspectives and valuable guidance. They can provide insights, advice, or alternative viewpoints that help us navigate difficult situations and make informed decisions. Having access to diverse perspectives broadens our understanding and opens up new possibilities.

Strategies for Seeking Emotional Support

1. Identify Trusted Individuals: Identify individuals in your life whom you trust and feel comfortable opening up to. These can be close friends, family members, partners, or mentors. Choose individuals who are empathetic, non-judgmental, and supportive.

2. Communicate Your Needs: Clearly communicate your need for emotional support to your trusted individuals. Let them know that you value their understanding and empathy. Be open and honest about your emotions and challenges, as this creates a space for genuine connection.

3. Seek Professional Support: Consider seeking support from trained professionals, such as therapists, counselors, or support groups. These professionals provide a safe and confidential environment for discussing your emotions, gaining insights, and developing coping strategies. Professional support offers specialized guidance and expertise.

4. Join Supportive Communities: Engage with support groups or communities that focus on similar experiences or challenges. These communities provide a space to share stories, receive empathy, and learn from others' journeys. Online platforms, local organizations, or therapy groups can connect you with individuals who understand your struggles.

5. Practice Active Listening: Cultivate your ability to actively listen to others. Offer your support and empathy when they share their emotions and experiences. By practicing active listening, you create an environment that encourages reciprocal emotional support within your relationships.

6. Utilize Helplines and Hotlines: In times of immediate need, consider reaching out to helplines or hotlines that provide emotional support. These services are staffed by trained professionals who can offer guidance, reassurance, and resources for managing stress. Helplines are available for various concerns, such as mental health, crisis situations, or specific life challenges.

Conclusion

Seeking emotional support is an essential aspect of managing stress and promoting emotional well-being. By identifying trusted individuals, communicating your needs, and seeking professional support when necessary, you can build a strong support network that offers understanding, empathy, and guidance. Remember, seeking emotional support is not a sign of weakness but a powerful tool for resilience and growth.

Technique 27: Joining Support Groups or Communities: Building Connections for Mutual Support and Empowerment

JOINING SUPPORT GROUPS or communities can be immensely beneficial for managing stress and promoting overall well-being. These groups provide a sense of belonging, understanding, and empowerment through shared experiences and mutual support. In this section, we explore the advantages of joining support groups or communities and provide guidance on how to find and engage with them effectively.

The Power of Support Groups or Communities

1. Shared Experiences: Support groups or communities consist of individuals who have experienced similar challenges or situations. Being part of a group where others understand your struggles can provide validation and reduce feelings of isolation. Shared experiences foster empathy, compassion, and a sense of camaraderie.

2. Emotional Support: Support groups or communities offer a safe space to express emotions, discuss concerns, and seek advice from individuals who can relate to your experiences. This emotional support can provide comfort, validation, and a sense of relief knowing that others are facing similar challenges.

3. Knowledge and Information: Support groups or communities provide opportunities for exchanging information, resources, and coping strategies. Members can share insights, tips, and personal experiences that may offer practical solutions or different perspectives on managing stress. Learning from others' journeys can expand your knowledge and empower you with new tools for stress management.

Strategies for Joining and Engaging with Support Groups or Communities

1. Research and Explore: Start by researching and exploring support groups or communities that align with your specific needs

or interests. Consider online platforms, local organizations, or social media groups that focus on topics related to stress management, mental health, personal development, or specific life challenges.

2. Assess Group Dynamics: Once you find potential support groups or communities, assess the group dynamics and values. Look for groups that foster a supportive, non-judgmental, and inclusive environment. Ensure that the group aligns with your personal values and provides a safe space for open and respectful discussions.

3. Participate Actively: Actively participate in group discussions and activities. Share your experiences, ask questions, and contribute to the conversations. Engage with others by offering support, empathy, and insights. Actively participating builds connections, strengthens the group's cohesion, and enhances the mutual support among members.

4. Respect Boundaries and Confidentiality: Respect the boundaries and confidentiality of the support group or community. Create a safe and trusting environment by maintaining confidentiality and refraining from sharing personal information or experiences outside the group unless explicitly permitted.

5. Seek Professional Guidance: While support groups or communities can provide valuable support, it's essential to remember that they are not a substitute for professional help. If you require professional guidance or therapy, consider seeking the support of qualified professionals who can offer specialized assistance alongside your participation in support groups.

6. Give and Receive Support: Embrace the spirit of reciprocity within the support group or community. Offer support, encouragement, and empathy to other members, just as you seek it for yourself. By giving and receiving support, you foster a sense of connection and contribute to the collective well-being of the group.

Conclusion

Joining support groups or communities can be a transformative experience for managing stress and finding a sense of belonging. By connecting with individuals who share similar experiences, you gain access to emotional support, practical knowledge, and a network of mutual empowerment. Engaging actively, respecting boundaries, and fostering a supportive environment will ensure a positive and enriching experience within the support group or community. Remember, you are not alone, and there is strength in seeking and offering support to others.

Technique 28: Setting Boundaries and Saying No: Empowering Yourself Through Healthy Limits

SETTING BOUNDARIES and learning to say no are vital skills for managing stress and maintaining a healthy balance in your life. By establishing clear boundaries and asserting your needs, you can protect your well-being, manage your time and energy effectively, and reduce stress caused by overwhelming commitments. In this section, we explore the importance of setting boundaries and provide practical strategies for saying no assertively and respectfully.

The Importance of Setting Boundaries

1. Protecting Your Well-being: Setting boundaries is an act of self-care that helps protect your physical, emotional, and mental well-being. It allows you to prioritize your needs, avoid burnout, and maintain a healthy work-life balance. By setting boundaries, you create space for rest, relaxation, and activities that bring you joy and fulfillment.

2. Maintaining Healthy Relationships: Boundaries are essential for fostering healthy relationships. They establish clear expectations, promote mutual respect, and prevent resentment or frustration from building up. Setting boundaries helps create harmonious and balanced interactions with others, enhancing the quality of your relationships.

3. Managing Stress: Boundaries play a significant role in managing stress by preventing overwhelm and excessive demands. When you

establish limits on your time, energy, and commitments, you can focus on what truly matters to you and allocate your resources effectively. Setting boundaries reduces the risk of becoming overwhelmed and promotes a sense of control over your life.

Strategies for Setting Boundaries and Saying No

1. Reflect on Your Needs: Take time to reflect on your needs, priorities, and values. Identify what is important to you and where you feel comfortable setting limits. Consider areas such as work, personal relationships, social engagements, and personal time. Understanding your needs will guide you in establishing appropriate boundaries.

2. Communicate Clearly: Clearly communicate your boundaries to others. Be honest and assertive in expressing your limits, needs, and expectations. Use "I" statements to express how certain situations or behaviors make you feel and explain the importance of your boundaries for your well-being.

3. Practice Self-Advocacy: Advocate for yourself by valuing your own needs and opinions. Recognize that it is okay to prioritize your well-being and say no when necessary. Stand firm in your boundaries, even if others may not initially understand or respect them. Remember that setting boundaries is an act of self-respect and self-care.

4. Use Assertive Language: Use assertive language when communicating your boundaries or saying no. Be firm, yet respectful and considerate. Practice phrases such as "I am not able to commit to that at this time," "I need some time to recharge," or "I appreciate your invitation, but I won't be able to attend." Avoid over-explaining or apologizing excessively for setting boundaries.

5. Set Clear Consequences: Establish clear consequences for boundary violations. Communicate what will happen if your boundaries are not respected, such as reducing contact, withdrawing from commitments, or seeking alternative solutions. Enforcing consequences reinforces the importance of your boundaries and encourages others to respect them.

6. Practice Self-Care: Prioritize self-care as an integral part of setting and maintaining boundaries. Engage in activities that promote relaxation, rejuvenation, and self-reflection. By taking care of yourself, you reinforce the importance of your boundaries and set a positive example for others.

Conclusion

Setting boundaries and learning to say no are empowering acts that allow you to protect your well-being, maintain healthy relationships, and effectively manage stress. By reflecting on your needs, communicating clearly, and practicing self-advocacy, you can establish boundaries that honor your values and priorities. Remember, setting boundaries is not selfish but essential for your overall health and happiness. Embrace the power of boundaries, and confidently say no when necessary to create a life that aligns with your truest self.

Chapter 8: Stress Reduction in the Workplace: Creating a Healthy and Productive Work Environment

Workplace stress can significantly impact your well-being and overall quality of life. Creating a healthy and supportive work environment is crucial for managing stress, promoting productivity, and fostering positive employee well-being. In this section, we explore strategies and techniques for reducing stress in the workplace, enabling you to thrive professionally and personally.

Recognizing Workplace Stress

1. Common Sources of Workplace Stress: Identify the common sources of stress in your workplace, such as high workload, tight deadlines, conflicts with colleagues, lack of autonomy, or inadequate resources. Understanding the specific stressors can help you develop targeted strategies for stress reduction.

2. Signs of Workplace Stress: Be aware of the signs and symptoms of workplace stress, which may include increased irritability, fatigue, difficulty concentrating, decreased motivation, and changes in sleep or appetite. Recognizing these signs can prompt proactive measures to address and alleviate stress.

Strategies for Stress Reduction in the Workplace

1. Foster Open Communication: Encourage open and honest communication in the workplace, creating an environment where employees feel comfortable expressing their concerns, seeking support, and sharing feedback. Effective communication channels promote collaboration, reduce misunderstandings, and mitigate potential stressors.

2. Establish Work-Life Balance: Promote work-life balance by setting clear boundaries between work and personal life. Encourage employees to take regular breaks, utilize their vacation time, and avoid excessive overtime. Flexibility in work schedules and remote work options, when feasible, can also contribute to a healthier work-life balance.

3. Promote a Positive Work Culture: Nurture a positive work culture that emphasizes appreciation, recognition, and mutual support. Encourage teamwork, celebrate achievements, and create opportunities for professional growth and development. Positive work environments foster motivation, job satisfaction, and resilience in the face of stress.

4. Provide Stress Management Resources: Offer stress management resources and tools to employees, such as workshops, seminars, or access to mental health support services. Provide information on stress reduction techniques, mindfulness practices, and relaxation exercises that employees can incorporate into their daily routines.

5. Encourage Physical Activity and Movement: Promote physical activity and movement in the workplace by providing access to exercise facilities, encouraging walking or standing meetings, and organizing wellness challenges or initiatives. Regular physical activity can reduce stress, boost mood, and improve overall well-being.

6. Implement Time Management Strategies: Support employees in managing their time effectively by encouraging priority setting, realistic goal setting, and efficient task organization. Provide training on time management techniques and tools, empowering employees to structure their workdays and allocate their time efficiently.

7. Support Social Connections: Foster social connections among employees by encouraging team-building activities, social events, and opportunities for collaboration. Creating a sense of community and belonging in the workplace can help alleviate stress, enhance job satisfaction, and improve overall well-being.

Conclusion

Reducing stress in the workplace is essential for creating a healthy and productive work environment. By recognizing workplace stressors, fostering open communication, promoting work-life balance, and providing stress management resources, employers and employees can work together to create a supportive and thriving workplace culture. Remember, a stress-free workplace benefits everyone involved, contributing to enhanced productivity, job satisfaction, and overall well-being.

Technique 29: Time Management Strategies: Maximizing Productivity and Minimizing Stress

EFFECTIVE TIME MANAGEMENT is key to maintaining a sense of control over your workload, increasing productivity, and reducing stress. By implementing proven time management strategies, you can make the most of your time, prioritize tasks effectively, and achieve a better work-life balance. In this section, we explore various time management techniques and strategies that will empower you to take control of your time and minimize stress.

Understanding Time Management

1. Importance of Time Management: Recognize the significance of time management in achieving personal and professional goals. Effective time management allows you to allocate your time wisely, focus on high-priority tasks, avoid procrastination, and create space for activities that bring you joy and fulfillment.

2. Benefits of Effective Time Management: Embrace the benefits of effective time management, such as reduced stress levels, increased productivity, improved efficiency, enhanced work-life balance, and a sense of accomplishment. By managing your time effectively, you can make progress towards your goals while maintaining a healthy and fulfilling lifestyle.

Time Management Strategies

1. Prioritize Tasks: Begin by identifying and prioritizing your tasks based on their urgency and importance. Use techniques like Eisenhower's Urgent-Important Matrix or the ABC method to categorize tasks into high, medium, and low priority. Focus on completing high-priority tasks first to ensure you tackle the most critical responsibilities.

2. Set Clear Goals: Set clear and specific goals for each day, week, or month. Define what you want to achieve and break down larger tasks into smaller, manageable steps. Clear goals provide direction and motivation, helping you stay focused and on track.

3. Create a Schedule: Develop a schedule or a to-do list to outline your tasks and allocate time for each activity. Utilize digital or physical planners, calendars, or task management apps to organize your schedule effectively. Be realistic in estimating the time needed for each task to avoid overloading your schedule.

4. Practice Time Blocking: Time blocking involves allocating specific blocks of time for different activities or task categories. Designate focused time blocks for important tasks, meetings, and creative work. This technique helps you manage interruptions, maintain focus, and enhance productivity.

5. Use Productivity Techniques: Explore productivity techniques such as the Pomodoro Technique, where you work in focused intervals followed by short breaks. This approach helps combat procrastination, improve concentration, and increase overall productivity.

6. Minimize Distractions: Identify and minimize distractions that hinder your productivity. Turn off notifications on your devices, close unnecessary tabs or applications, and create a dedicated work environment that is free from distractions. Consider utilizing productivity tools that block distracting websites or apps during specified work periods.

7. Delegate and Outsource: Learn to delegate tasks that can be handled by others, whether it's assigning work to colleagues or hiring

freelancers or professionals for specific tasks. Delegating allows you to focus on high-priority responsibilities and reduces your workload, freeing up time for more essential tasks.

8. Practice Time Flexibility: Embrace the concept of time flexibility, recognizing that unforeseen events or interruptions may occur. Allow some buffer time in your schedule to accommodate unexpected tasks or delays. Being adaptable and flexible in managing your time helps reduce stress and maintain a balanced approach.

9. Reflect and Adjust: Regularly reflect on your time management strategies and assess their effectiveness. Identify areas for improvement and make necessary adjustments to your schedule or techniques. Continuous evaluation and adaptation will help optimize your time management practices over time.

Conclusion

By implementing effective time management strategies, you can take control of your time, increase productivity, and reduce stress. Prioritize tasks, set clear goals, create a schedule, and practice techniques like time blocking and minimizing distractions. Remember, time management is a skill that requires practice and self-awareness. By mastering these strategies, you can make the most of your time, achieve your goals, and lead a more balanced and fulfilling life.

Technique 30: Work-Life Balance: Finding Harmony and Fulfillment in All Areas of Life

ACHIEVING A HEALTHY work-life balance is essential for overall well-being and satisfaction. Balancing the demands of work with personal life commitments can help reduce stress, enhance relationships, and foster a sense of fulfillment. In this section, we explore strategies and techniques to achieve work-life balance, enabling you to prioritize self-care, nurture relationships, and find harmony in all areas of your life.

Understanding Work-Life Balance

1. What is Work-Life Balance? Define work-life balance as the equilibrium between professional obligations and personal life responsibilities. It involves allocating time and energy to various domains, such as work, family, relationships, self-care, and leisure activities, in a way that aligns with your values and priorities.

2. The Importance of Work-Life Balance: Recognize the significance of work-life balance in maintaining physical and mental well-being. A balanced approach allows you to avoid burnout, enhance productivity, nurture relationships, and pursue personal interests outside of work.

Strategies for Achieving Work-Life Balance

1. Set Boundaries: Establish clear boundaries between work and personal life. Define specific work hours and limit work-related activities during non-work hours. Communicate your boundaries to colleagues and clients, and strive to disconnect from work-related devices and notifications outside of designated work hours.

2. Prioritize Self-Care: Make self-care a non-negotiable aspect of your routine. Dedicate time for activities that promote physical, mental, and emotional well-being, such as exercise, meditation, hobbies, and relaxation. Prioritizing self-care replenishes your energy and helps you better manage work and personal commitments.

3. Delegate and Outsource: Learn to delegate tasks and responsibilities, both at work and in personal life, when possible. Identify tasks that can be outsourced or shared with others, freeing up time and reducing overwhelm. Delegating allows you to focus on activities that align with your strengths and priorities.

4. Practice Effective Time Management: Utilize time management techniques, such as prioritization, scheduling, and task organization, to optimize your productivity. Allocate time for work tasks, personal activities, and relationships, ensuring that each area receives the

attention it deserves. Effective time management helps prevent work from encroaching on personal time and vice versa.

5. Communicate and Negotiate Flexibility: Openly communicate with your employer or supervisor about your work-life balance needs. Explore flexible work arrangements, such as remote work options, flexible hours, or compressed workweeks, if feasible. Negotiating for flexibility enables you to better manage work and personal commitments.

6. Nurture Relationships: Cultivate meaningful relationships with family, friends, and loved ones. Dedicate quality time to connect, engage, and create memories with the important people in your life. Building and maintaining strong relationships enhances overall well-being and provides a support network during challenging times.

7. Practice Mindfulness: Incorporate mindfulness practices into your daily routine. Engage in activities with full presence and awareness, whether it's during work tasks, conversations, or leisure activities. Mindfulness helps you savor the present moment, reduce stress, and enhance overall satisfaction.

8. Embrace Leisure and Recreation: Make time for leisure and recreational activities that bring you joy and fulfillment. Engage in hobbies, pursue interests, and participate in activities that allow you to relax, recharge, and experience pleasure outside of work responsibilities.

9. Seek Support: Don't hesitate to seek support when needed. Reach out to trusted friends, family members, or professionals for guidance, advice, or assistance. Seeking support helps alleviate stress, gain perspective, and share the load in challenging times.

Conclusion

Achieving work-life balance is a continuous journey that requires conscious effort and self-reflection. By setting boundaries, prioritizing self-care, practicing effective time management, nurturing relationships, and seeking support, you can create a harmonious and fulfilling balance between work and personal life. Remember, work-life balance is not about perfect equilibrium but finding a dynamic integration that aligns with your values and priorities.

Technique 31: Stress-Relief Techniques during Breaks: Recharge and Rejuvenate for Optimal Productivity

TAKING REGULAR BREAKS throughout the workday is essential for managing stress, maintaining focus, and maximizing productivity. By incorporating stress-relief techniques into your breaks, you can recharge your energy, reduce tension, and promote overall well-being. In this section, we explore various techniques that you can practice during your breaks to alleviate stress and enhance your workday experience.

Understanding the Importance of Breaks

1. The Role of Breaks in Stress Management: Breaks play a crucial role in stress management by allowing you to step away from work tasks and recharge both physically and mentally. Taking regular breaks helps prevent burnout, boosts productivity, improves concentration, and enhances overall well-being.

2. Benefits of Stress-Relief Techniques during Breaks: Incorporating stress-relief techniques into your breaks offers numerous benefits, including reduced stress levels, increased relaxation, improved mood, enhanced focus and concentration, and a renewed sense of energy. These techniques provide a much-needed opportunity to reset and rejuvenate during the workday.

Stress-Relief Techniques during Breaks

1. Deep Breathing Exercises: Practice deep breathing exercises during your breaks to induce a state of relaxation and calm. Take slow, deep breaths, inhaling through your nose and exhaling through your

mouth. Focus on the sensation of your breath, allowing it to slow down and deepen, helping to reduce stress and promote relaxation.

2. Stretching and Physical Movement: Engage in gentle stretching exercises or take a short walk during your breaks. Stretching helps release tension in your muscles and promotes blood circulation, while physical movement stimulates endorphin release, improving your mood and energy levels.

3. Mindfulness Meditation: Spend a few minutes practicing mindfulness meditation during your breaks. Find a quiet space, sit comfortably, and bring your attention to the present moment. Focus on your breath, bodily sensations, or simply observe your thoughts without judgment. Mindfulness meditation helps calm the mind, reduce stress, and enhance mental clarity.

4. Visualizations and Imagery: Use your breaks as an opportunity for guided visualizations or positive imagery exercises. Close your eyes and imagine yourself in a peaceful, serene setting or visualize accomplishing a goal or overcoming a challenge. This technique allows you to mentally escape stressors and promote a sense of calm and optimism.

5. Relaxation Techniques: Explore various relaxation techniques, such as progressive muscle relaxation or guided relaxation audios, during your breaks. These techniques involve systematically tensing and releasing different muscle groups or following a guided relaxation script, helping to release physical and mental tension.

6. Engage in a Pleasant Activity: Dedicate your breaks to activities that bring you joy and relaxation. Listen to calming music, read a few pages of a book, engage in a creative hobby, or engage in a brief mindfulness exercise like coloring or doodling. Engaging in pleasant activities during breaks can help shift your focus away from work-related stress and promote a sense of enjoyment.

7. Social Connection: Use your breaks to connect with colleagues or loved ones. Engage in a brief conversation, share a laugh, or connect

through phone calls or video chats. Social connection during breaks helps foster a sense of support, belonging, and camaraderie, reducing stress and enhancing well-being.

8. Refresh with Water and Healthy Snacks: Hydrate your body and nourish yourself with healthy snacks during your breaks. Drinking water helps rehydrate your body and promote mental clarity, while consuming nutritious snacks provides sustained energy and supports overall well-being.

Conclusion

Incorporating stress-relief techniques during your breaks is crucial for managing stress, promoting well-being, and optimizing productivity. Whether it's deep breathing exercises, stretching, mindfulness meditation, visualizations, engaging in pleasant activities, or fostering social connections, finding the right combination of techniques can help you recharge and rejuvenate during your breaks, leading to a more balanced and fulfilling workday experience. Remember, taking care of your well-being during breaks is an investment in your overall performance and satisfaction.

Technique 32: Effective Communication and Conflict Resolution: Building Positive Relationships in the Workplace

EFFECTIVE COMMUNICATION and conflict resolution skills are essential for maintaining a harmonious work environment and reducing stress levels. Clear and open communication promotes understanding, collaboration, and the resolution of conflicts in a productive manner. In this section, we explore techniques and strategies for improving communication and resolving conflicts effectively, enabling you to foster positive relationships and reduce stress in the workplace.

Understanding Effective Communication

1. Importance of Effective Communication: Effective communication is the foundation of healthy work relationships. It facilitates clarity, understanding, and collaboration among team members, reduces misunderstandings and conflicts, and promotes a positive and inclusive work culture.

2. Active Listening: Active listening is a crucial component of effective communication. It involves giving your full attention to the speaker, seeking to understand their perspective, and providing appropriate responses. By practicing active listening, you can foster empathy, build trust, and establish stronger connections with your colleagues.

Improving Communication Skills

1. Clear and Concise Expression: Strive to express yourself clearly and concisely in both written and verbal communication. Use simple language, organize your thoughts, and be mindful of your tone and body language. Clear communication helps avoid misunderstandings and promotes effective collaboration.

2. Respectful and Constructive Feedback: Offer feedback and critique in a respectful and constructive manner. Focus on specific behaviors or issues, provide examples, and offer suggestions for improvement. Constructive feedback helps foster a growth-oriented culture and contributes to personal and professional development.

3. Nonverbal Communication: Pay attention to your nonverbal cues, such as facial expressions, body language, and gestures, as they play a significant role in communication. Maintain eye contact, use open and welcoming body language, and be aware of how your nonverbal signals may be interpreted by others.

Conflict Resolution Strategies

1. Identify the Issue: Clearly define the conflict or issue at hand. Identify the underlying interests, needs, or concerns of all parties involved. This step helps create a shared understanding of the problem and paves the way for a constructive resolution.

2. Active Listening and Empathy: Engage in active listening and demonstrate empathy when engaging in conflict resolution. Listen attentively to each party's perspective, seek to understand their emotions and concerns, and validate their experiences. Empathy fosters a sense of connection and enables a more collaborative resolution.

3. Find Common Ground: Identify areas of agreement or shared goals among the conflicting parties. Focus on finding common ground and building upon those shared interests. This approach helps shift the focus from differences to areas of alignment, promoting a more cooperative resolution.

4. Generate Solutions: Encourage brainstorming and generate multiple potential solutions to the conflict. Encourage open and honest communication, and consider all perspectives when exploring possible resolutions. Strive for win-win outcomes that address the concerns of all parties involved.

5. Collaborative Decision-Making: Involve all relevant parties in the decision-making process. Encourage collaboration, seek consensus, and make decisions that are fair and mutually beneficial. Collaborative decision-making promotes ownership and commitment to the resolution.

6. Seek Mediation if Needed: If the conflict persists or becomes challenging to resolve, consider involving a neutral third party as a mediator. Mediators can help facilitate communication, guide the resolution process, and assist in finding a mutually agreeable solution.

CONCLUSION

Effective communication and conflict resolution skills are crucial for maintaining positive relationships and reducing stress in the workplace. By practicing active listening, improving communication skills, and adopting effective conflict resolution strategies, you can create a supportive and collaborative work environment. Remember, open and respectful communication lays the foundation for healthy work relationships and contributes to a more harmonious and productive work environment.

Chapter 9: Strategies for Long-Term Stress Management: Building Resilience and Sustaining Well-being

Long-term stress management is essential for maintaining overall well-being and preventing chronic stress-related health issues. It involves adopting proactive strategies that build resilience, promote self-care, and foster a healthy lifestyle. In this section, we explore various strategies that can help you manage stress in the long run, enabling you to sustain well-being and thrive in all aspects of your life.

Technique 33: Building Resilience: Strengthening Your Ability to Thrive in the Face of Stress

BUILDING RESILIENCE is key to effectively managing and navigating stress in the long term. Resilience refers to the ability to bounce back from challenges, adapt to adversity, and maintain a positive outlook despite difficult circumstances. In this section, we explore strategies and techniques that can help you cultivate resilience, enhance your coping skills, and thrive in the face of stress.

1. Developing a Growth Mindset

1.1 Embracing Challenges: View challenges as opportunities for growth and learning rather than insurmountable obstacles. Embrace a mindset that believes in your ability to overcome difficulties and learn valuable lessons from them.

1.2 Cultivating Optimism: Practice cultivating a positive outlook and optimism, even during challenging times. Focus on possibilities, practice gratitude, and reframe setbacks as temporary and solvable.

1.3 Embracing Failure as a Learning Opportunity: Shift your perspective on failure and setbacks. See them as opportunities for growth, learning, and self-improvement. Analyze what went wrong, learn from the experience, and apply those lessons in future endeavors.

2. Building Strong Social Connections

2.1 Developing Supportive Relationships: Cultivate a network of supportive relationships with friends, family, colleagues, or support groups. Surround yourself with individuals who provide encouragement, empathy, and understanding during difficult times.

2.2 Seeking and Offering Support: Don't hesitate to seek support when you need it. Reach out to others and share your feelings and concerns. Similarly, offer support to others who may be going through challenging times. Helping others can also strengthen your own resilience.

2.3 Engaging in Social Activities: Participate in social activities that promote connection, such as group hobbies, community events, or volunteering. Engaging in shared experiences and connecting with others fosters a sense of belonging and support.

3. Cultivating Emotional Well-being

3.1 Practicing Self-Compassion: Be kind and understanding to yourself during challenging times. Treat yourself with the same compassion and care that you would offer to a friend. Practice self-compassion through positive self-talk, self-care activities, and self-reflection.

3.2 Managing Stress: Implement stress management techniques, such as mindfulness, relaxation exercises, and regular self-care practices. Take breaks when needed, engage in activities that bring you joy, and prioritize self-care to maintain emotional well-being.

3.3 Emotion Regulation: Develop skills for effectively managing and regulating your emotions. Practice techniques such as deep breathing, journaling, or talking to a trusted confidant to process and navigate challenging emotions.

4. Enhancing Problem-Solving Skills

4.1 Identifying Solutions: When faced with a problem or challenge, break it down into smaller, more manageable components. Identify potential solutions and evaluate their feasibility. Consider seeking input from others who may offer different perspectives.

4.2 Taking Action: Once you have identified potential solutions, take action and implement them. Start with small steps and adjust your approach as needed. Taking proactive steps to address challenges empowers you and increases your sense of control.

4.3 Learning from Setbacks: Embrace setbacks as learning opportunities. Analyze what went wrong, reflect on the lessons learned, and use that knowledge to refine your problem-solving skills for future challenges.

Conclusion

Building resilience is a lifelong process that involves developing a growth mindset, building strong social connections, cultivating emotional well-being, and enhancing problem-solving skills. By incorporating these strategies into your life, you can strengthen your ability to thrive in the face of stress, bounce back from setbacks, and maintain a positive outlook. Remember, resilience is a skill that can be developed and nurtured, leading to increased well-being and overall life satisfaction.

Technique 34: Self-Care and Self-Compassion: Nurturing Your Well-being

SELF-CARE AND SELF-compassion are essential components of long-term stress management. They involve prioritizing your own needs, practicing kindness towards yourself, and nurturing your overall well-being. In this section, we explore strategies and practices that can help you cultivate self-care and self-compassion, enabling you to sustain your well-being and navigate the challenges of life with greater resilience.

Prioritizing Self-Care

- Physical Self-Care: Take care of your physical well-being by engaging in activities that promote good health. This includes regular exercise, eating nutritious foods, getting enough sleep, and practicing good hygiene habits. Prioritize activities that rejuvenate and energize your body.

- Emotional Self-Care: Attend to your emotional well-being by acknowledging and expressing your feelings in healthy ways. Engage in activities that bring you joy and comfort, such as pursuing hobbies, spending time with loved ones, journaling, or engaging in creative outlets.

- Mental Self-Care: Nourish your mind by engaging in activities that stimulate and challenge you intellectually. This can include reading books, learning new skills, solving puzzles or brain games, or engaging in mindful activities that promote mental clarity and relaxation.

- Spiritual Self-Care: Cultivate a sense of purpose and connection by engaging in activities that align with your values and beliefs. This can involve practicing meditation, mindfulness, prayer, spending time in nature, or engaging in activities that bring a sense of inner peace and transcendence.

Practicing Self-Compassion

- Kind Self-Talk: Be mindful of the way you speak to yourself. Replace self-critical and judgmental thoughts with kind, supportive, and encouraging self-talk. Treat yourself with the same compassion and understanding that you would offer to a close friend.

- Acceptance of Imperfections: Embrace your imperfections and accept that nobody is perfect. Allow yourself to make mistakes and view them as opportunities for growth and learning. Practice self-acceptance and let go of the need for perfection.

- Setting Boundaries: Learn to set healthy boundaries that protect your time, energy, and well-being. Say no to excessive demands or obligations that overwhelm you and prioritize self-care activities. Respecting your own boundaries is an act of self-compassion.

- Self-Reflection and Self-Discovery: Engage in self-reflection to gain deeper insight into your needs, desires, and values. Explore activities that promote self-discovery, such as journaling, mindfulness, or seeking the support of a therapist or coach. Understanding yourself better can lead to greater self-compassion.

Cultivating Mindfulness

- Present-Moment Awareness: Practice being fully present in the current moment, without judgment or attachment to past or future thoughts. Engage in mindfulness meditation, body scan exercises, or mindful walking to cultivate a greater sense of presence and reduce stress.

- Self-Awareness: Develop a heightened sense of self-awareness by paying attention to your thoughts, emotions, and physical sensations. Notice any patterns or triggers that contribute to stress and use this awareness to respond with self-compassion and self-care.

- Mindful Self-Compassion: Combine mindfulness with self-compassion by directing loving-kindness and acceptance towards yourself. Practice self-compassionate meditation or engage in activities that evoke feelings of compassion and kindness towards yourself.

Conclusion

Self-care and self-compassion are vital practices for maintaining long-term well-being and effectively managing stress. By prioritizing self-care activities, nurturing self-compassion, and cultivating mindfulness, you can develop a stronger foundation for resilience and navigate life's challenges with greater ease. Remember, taking care of yourself is not selfish but rather essential for leading a balanced, fulfilling, and stress-free life.

Technique 35: Mindset Shifts and Positive Psychology: Cultivating a Positive Outlook

OUR MINDSET PLAYS A significant role in how we perceive and respond to stress. By cultivating a positive mindset and incorporating principles from positive psychology, we can effectively manage stress and enhance our overall well-being. In this section, we explore mindset shifts and practices that promote a positive outlook and empower us to navigate life's challenges with resilience and optimism.

1. Embracing a Growth Mindset

A growth mindset is the belief that our abilities and intelligence can be developed through dedication and effort. By adopting a growth mindset, we view challenges as opportunities for growth and learning rather than obstacles. This mindset shift allows us to embrace failures as valuable lessons and persist in the face of setbacks.

2. Cultivating Gratitude

Practicing gratitude involves intentionally focusing on the positive aspects of our lives and expressing appreciation for them. It shifts our attention away from stressors and cultivates a sense of abundance and contentment. Engaging in gratitude journaling, expressing gratitude to others, or simply reflecting on things we are grateful for can significantly reduce stress and enhance well-being.

3. Reframing and Positive Perspective

Reframing is the practice of consciously shifting our perspective on challenging situations. It involves identifying and challenging negative thought patterns and replacing them with more positive and empowering interpretations. By reframing our thoughts, we can change our emotional responses and find new solutions to problems.

4. Cultivating Optimism

Optimism is the belief that positive outcomes are possible, even in difficult circumstances. Cultivating optimism involves focusing on the potential for growth, finding silver linings in challenging situations, and maintaining a hopeful attitude. Optimistic individuals tend to experience lower levels of stress and greater resilience in the face of adversity.

5. Practicing Self-Compassion

Self-compassion involves extending kindness, understanding, and acceptance towards oneself, particularly during times of stress or failure. It entails treating ourselves with the same compassion we would offer to a loved one. By practicing self-compassion, we can reduce self-criticism, build resilience, and enhance our overall well-being.

6. Positive Self-Talk and Affirmations

Positive self-talk involves consciously directing supportive and encouraging statements towards ourselves. By replacing negative self-talk with positive affirmations, we can cultivate a more optimistic and empowering inner dialogue. Positive self-talk enhances our self-belief, reduces stress, and increases our ability to cope with challenges.

7. Engaging in Acts of Kindness

Acts of kindness towards others have been shown to have a positive impact on our own well-being. Engaging in acts of kindness, such as volunteering, helping others, or practicing random acts of kindness, not only benefits those we assist but also boosts our own mood and reduces stress.

Conclusion

By cultivating a positive mindset and incorporating principles from positive psychology into our lives, we can effectively manage stress and enhance our overall well-being. Embracing a growth mindset, practicing gratitude, reframing challenges, cultivating optimism, practicing self-compassion, engaging in positive self-talk, and performing acts of kindness all contribute to a positive outlook and increased resilience. Remember, mindset shifts require practice and persistence, but the benefits are well worth the effort.

Conclusion

In conclusion, stress management is crucial for maintaining a healthy and balanced life in today's fast-paced world. This ebook, "Stress Management: 40 Transformative Techniques to Prevent and Reduce Everyday Stress in Your Life," provides a comprehensive guide to help you navigate and overcome stress effectively.

Throughout the ebook, we have explored various techniques and strategies to manage stress in different areas of life. From understanding the causes and effects of stress to implementing mindfulness and meditation practices, from adopting healthy lifestyle habits to utilizing cognitive strategies and seeking social support, each chapter offers valuable insights and practical tools to empower you in your stress management journey.

Remember, stress is a normal part of life, but how we respond to it determines its impact on our well-being. By implementing the techniques and practices outlined in this ebook, you can build resilience, improve your overall quality of life, and prevent stress from overwhelming you.

It is my sincere hope that this ebook serves as a valuable resource for you in your pursuit of stress-free living. May it provide you with the knowledge, inspiration, and tools necessary to prevent and reduce everyday stress, enabling you to live a more fulfilling and balanced life.

Dedicate yourself to self-care, self-compassion, and the cultivation of positive mindset shifts. Embrace the transformative power of these techniques and make them a part of your daily life. Remember, you have the power to manage and reduce stress, and by doing so, you can unlock your full potential and create a life of greater joy, well-being, and fulfillment.

Wishing you a stress-free and empowered journey ahead!

Additional Books and Resources

1. "THE RELAXATION and Stress Reduction Workbook" by Martha Davis, Elizabeth Robbins Eshelman, and Matthew McKay - This workbook provides a wealth of practical techniques and exercises for managing stress, including relaxation techniques, cognitive strategies, and lifestyle changes.

2. "Full Catastrophe Living: Using the Wisdom of Your Body and Mind to Face Stress, Pain, and Illness" by Jon Kabat-Zinn - This book introduces the concept of mindfulness-based stress reduction (MBSR) and offers guidance on incorporating mindfulness into daily life to reduce stress and enhance well-being.

3. "The Upside of Stress: Why Stress Is Good for You, and How to Get Good at It" by Kelly McGonigal - In this book, the author challenges the common belief that stress is always harmful and provides a fresh perspective on how stress can be harnessed as a positive force for growth and resilience.

4. "The Power of Now: A Guide to Spiritual Enlightenment" by Eckhart Tolle - While not specifically focused on stress management, this book offers profound insights on living in the present moment and cultivating inner peace, which can have a transformative effect on how we perceive and respond to stress.

5. "Burnout: The Secret to Unlocking the Stress Cycle" by Emily Nagoski and Amelia Nagoski - This book explores the concept of burnout and offers practical strategies for completing the stress cycle, managing overwhelm, and restoring well-being.

6. "Daring Greatly: How the Courage to Be Vulnerable Transforms the Way We Live, Love, Parent, and Lead" by Brené Brown - This book addresses the underlying factors contributing to stress, such as

shame and vulnerability, and offers insights on cultivating resilience, authenticity, and wholehearted living.

7. Online Resources: Websites like the American Psychological Association (www.apa.org) and Mindful (www.mindful.org) provide a wealth of articles, research, and resources on stress management, mindfulness, and well-being. Additionally, mobile apps like Headspace and Calm offer guided meditations and relaxation exercises to support stress reduction.

Remember to adapt and customize the techniques and strategies to fit your unique needs and preferences. Exploring these additional books and resources will further deepen your understanding of stress management and provide additional tools to support your journey toward a healthier, happier, and more stress-free life.

About the Author

Hello, I'm Rami, and I'm thrilled to share with you my passion for mindfulness, psychology, and personal growth. With a Master's degree in Psychology and a deep understanding of the human mind, I have dedicated my career to helping individuals cultivate a sense of inner peace, clarity, and fulfillment.

As an advocate for mindful living, I believe that true transformation begins from within. Through my studies and personal experiences, I have witnessed the profound impact that mindfulness can have on our well-being and overall quality of life. It is my mission to empower others to tap into their inner wisdom, break free from self-limiting patterns, and create a more meaningful and authentic existence.

Beyond my academic background, I am also an ardent advocate for conscious living and ethical choices. As a committed vegan, I embrace a lifestyle that promotes compassion, respect for all beings, and sustainable living. I strongly believe that our choices have the power to create a positive impact not only on our own lives but also on the world around us.

Through this book, I aim to provide you with practical tools, insights, and techniques that will guide you on a transformative journey toward a more mindful and stress-free life. I draw upon my knowledge of psychology, mindfulness practices, and personal experiences to offer you a comprehensive roadmap for navigating the challenges of overthinking, finding inner peace, and embracing the present moment.

My hope is that this book serves as a source of inspiration, guidance, and empowerment as you embark on your own path of self-discovery and personal growth. Together, let's unlock the secrets to mindful living and create a life of greater clarity, joy, and fulfillment.

With warmest wishes,

Rami

Don't miss out!

Visit the website below and you can sign up to receive emails whenever Rami Georgiev publishes a new book. There's no charge and no obligation.

https://books2read.com/r/B-A-JXNW-WSELC

BOOKS 2 READ

Connecting independent readers to independent writers.

Did you love *Stress Management: 35 Transformative Techniques to Prevent and Reduce Everyday Stress in Your Life*? Then you should read *Embracing the Unvarnished Truth: 40 Truths About Human Relationships*[1] by Rami Georgiev!

[2]

"Embracing the Unvarnished Truth: 40 Truths About Human Relationships" is a brutally honest exploration of the intricacies and challenges that lie within our connections with others. In this thought-provoking book, the author fearlessly uncovers the raw realities of love, trust, communication, intimacy, conflict, and personal growth. With deep insights and engaging storytelling, the book delves into 40 profound truths that underpin the human experience of relationships. Drawing from psychology, personal anecdotes, and real-life examples, this book offers a candid and enlightening

1. https://books2read.com/u/bOP0ON

2. https://books2read.com/u/bOP0ON

perspective on the complexities of human relationships. It serves as a guide for those seeking to navigate the highs and lows of relationships with authenticity, resilience, and self-awareness. "Embracing the Unvarnished Truth" invites readers to challenge societal norms, confront uncomfortable truths, and embark on a transformative journey towards healthier, more fulfilling connections.

Read more at vegandelights.space.

www.ingramcontent.com/pod-product-compliance
Lightning Source LLC
LaVergne TN
LVHW090419210926
848480LV00002B/622
* 9 7 9 8 2 2 3 7 2 5 0 6 0 *